Jac
Me

OF CHINA

D0479645

DATE DUE			

Arts and Crafts of China

SCOTT MINICK AND JIAO PING

with 183 illustrations,
147 in color

Frontispiece *Miniature mask carved in the style of those used in the* Di xi, *or operatic performances of Guizhou Province. h.16 cm*

Designed by Liz Rudderham

First published in the United States of America in 1996 by
Thames and Hudson Inc.,
500 Fifth Avenue, New York, New York 10110

Library of Congress Catalog Card Number 96-60238
ISBN 0-500-27896-2

Printed in Singapore

CONTENTS

PREFACE

The documentation of China's arts and crafts traditions is a formidable task, richly deserved and seldom ventured. This book is by no means an exhaustive study, rather a sampling of current arts and crafts activity. As with any research in a country so vast, what one finds at any particular moment in any given place is largely a matter of luck and the benevolent will of the gods. As a consequence, the visitor to China may still expect to find many noteworthy objects not represented in these pages. In an effort to present many of the lesser-known crafts, which have gone relatively unrecorded, we have at the same time chosen to omit many objects on which there have already been significant studies. Published works on Chinese jade carving, furniture, basketry, snuff bottles,

porcelains and cloisonné are already substantial; each is important in the grand artistic traditions of the country, but they should not figure prominently in a book primarily devoted to the less-recognized, more folk-oriented handicrafts.

We would like to thank the many people who so generously opened their homes and workshops to us during our research and who contributed their special knowledge when documentary evidence ran thin. Special acknowledgments are due to Mr Liu Yun for allowing us to photograph numerous Di and Nuo masks from his extraordinary collection and for the knowledge he shared with us on Miao minority crafts, and to the family of Mr Tai Liping who so graciously welcomed us into their home and printmaking studio after we

arrived unannounced. Thanks are also extended to Mr Guo Miao for his valued insights on craft activity in and around Beijing; Diane Deyo and Nicholas Kripal for their expertise on artisanal weaving and ceramics methodology; and Mr Du Zheng Jun for geographic guidance in provinces where we might otherwise have been hopelessly lost.

Furthermore, a very special debt of gratitude is due to the many thousands of anonymous Chinese artisans who have devoted endless hours and patience to producing the fine objects illustrated here. May their admirable sense of beauty, tradition and craftsmanship provide inspiration for generations to come.

Traditional calligraphy materials include carved bamboo brushes, which often bear auspicious inscriptions. Elaborate ink sticks are ground with water in the artist's inkstone to obtain the desired fluidity. An assortment of carved stone 'chops', or seals, is used to sign a work with the artist's name or a poetic inscription.

Hand-coloured woodblock print of Lu Ban, the legendary carpenter, whose tremendous feats of ingenious architectural construction and fine craftsmanship became legendary throughout China, leading to his eventual immortalization as the patron saint of carpenters and builders. 48 x 43 cm

ORIGINS

Heaven has its times,
Earth its weather,
bamboo its beauty,
and work its craftsmanship;
combine these four and you can achieve the good

– Kao Gong Ji
(China's earliest written record on handicrafts)

China is a land of extraordinarily vibrant geographic, cultural and linguistic diversity. Its current population exceeds 1.2 billion people, comprising 55 ethnic minorities in addition to the Han majority that represents 92 per cent of the country. Among this already heterogeneous mix of ethnic identities, hundreds of local and regional dialects further differentiate the population by geographic situation. China's vast landscape spans 9.6 million square kilometres, with a topographic range that includes the parched Taklamakan Desert in the northwestern province of Xinjiang, the wild and expansive grasslands of Inner Mongolia, the misty pine-covered mountains in Anhui, the luxuriant bamboo forests of Sichuan and the majestic palm groves in Yunnan's tropical south. The overall effect of this tremendous variegation on Chinese arts and crafts is readily apparent as one travels from province to province. Local materials dictate both form and function in provincial craft communities. The yellow earth of Shaanxi has long supplied peasants with the raw clay to make a fascinating variety of festive toys, while the dense bamboo forests of Sichuan provide for hundreds of woven handicrafts and practical items for daily use.

Today's China is a land of enormous contrasts, simultaneously chaotic and harmonious. Perpetually overcrowded, yet prosperous, its cities are constantly abuzz with an inexhaustible flurry of people seeking to make their fortunes. The countryside, while breathtakingly beautiful, often verges on environmental exhaustion. Endowed with an artistic patrimony perhaps unmatched in the world, the average Chinese has almost no interest in anything hinting of age or suggestive of the country's long dynastic past. These are

Late nineteenth-century pedlars of small crafts and household goods. Guangdong Province.

only a few of the paradoxes now found in China, each of which may be better understood by looking at the underlying philosophical currents that have guided Chinese life for thousands of years.

In the ancient canonical treatise, *The Book of Changes*, all wordly and cosmological relationships are defined as being in a perpetual state of flux, unfixed and forever changing. Permanent creation is only born through the harnessing of the

Amulet based on an ancient coin design bearing the Ba gua *or 'Eight Triagrams', the foundation for the* Yi Jing *(I-Ching). The* Ba gua *represent the eight natural phenomena of heaven, earth, thunder, wind, water, fire, mountains and rivers. At the centre is the symbol of* yin *and* yang, *which – through their delicate balance of opposites – strive to maintain harmony and order.*

opposing forces known as *yin* and *yang*, which must constantly struggle to maintain a proper balance. The *yin* is defined as all that is cool, dark, female and earthly. The *yang* represents that which is hot, bright, male and astral. Together they form an organic union whose perfect harmony is wholly dependent on their fundamental contrasts. Seen in this context, the seemingly discordant nature of much of modern China is neither a recent, nor necessarily a negative, characteristic of an ancient land. The delicate balance of opposites is an intrinsic component of Chinese life that has produced continuous cycles of renaissance and revolution for thousands of years.

The fundamental belief in the *yin* and the *yang* remains a pervasive concept in the Chinese search for spiritual and physical harmony. It is deeply embedded in the routines and lifestyles of the people, governing the balance of the daily diet, the condition of the physical body and even the dynamics of the home and workplace. This supreme cosmological order underlies each and every creative act and remains the primary concern of the classical artist in search of aesthetic perfection. The *yin* and the *yang* constitute the root of creative expression and manifest themselves in every gesture of the brush, each manipulation of clay or sculpting of stone. They are an omnipresent concern, even extending to the selection of the creative materials themselves.

In the case of the folk artist or artisan, the recognition and interpretation of these cosmic forces operates on a far more intuitive level, free of philosophical deliberation. Nevertheless, the artisan's own underlying need to transcend both physical and material limitations to achieve a greater spiritual harmony is equally evident, even in the most humble of rural crafts. Such works, unfettered by formal

training, are imbued with a natural and expressive vibrancy, joining local beliefs and materials in an ongoing exploration of the mysterious forces that guide human destiny.

Among China's rural people and ethnic minorities, superstition and traditional lore deeply affect everyday thoughts and practices. Ancient concerns for health, happiness and good fortune have led to an abundance of ceremonies intended to appease the gods and honour the deceased. This is particularly evident during festival periods, when elaborate handicraft offerings are prepared in honour of the many spirits and demons that govern the diverse facets of their lives. Not only do these forces have the power to grant a family happiness and good fortune, they may also bring regrettable calamity and suffering through improper or insufficient recognition during the year. Thus, local folk artists are regularly called upon to produce reverential offerings with the full knowledge that the quality of their work will not only affect the health and prosperity of their own family, but also that of the other villagers as well.

The climax for most craft activity is centred around the numerous festivals corresponding to the ancient lunar calendar. They represent the culmination of many months of preparation and explode in lavish ceremonies featuring special foods, musical performances and expressive dances, which serve to unite young and old in an understanding and perpetuation of the community's ancient beliefs. The most widely celebrated among China's diverse population are the Spring, Pure Brightness, Dragon Boat and Full Moon festivals. At these times, local artisans display and sell a variety of craftwork, including clothing embroidered with symbols to ward off evil, scented sachets to prevent sickness, intricate paper cuts to bring good fortune, woodblock prints to guard the home and elaborately painted clay toys to entertain and protect the local children.

Such rural crafts reveal much about contemporary village life. They are not simply nostalgic souvenirs of another era, but rather symbols of continuity that with each succeeding generation reflect the ideas and values of an entire community in transition. In this manner the folk arts and crafts of a village become a virtual mirror of its daily existence. When an object no longer serves its intended ceremonial or functional role, its production and use fade away. As a result of such dedication to purpose, Chinese crafts have remained resistant over many centuries to the notion of change simply for the sake of change.

Furthermore, a well-developed network of trade from a very early date assured a degree of prosperity and even fame for many of China's minority cultures and provinces producing specialized handicrafts. Merchants plying the Silk Road and traders sailing the South China Sea found enthusiastic markets throughout Southeast Asia and eventually Europe for a variety of Chinese goods. Trade between the minority peoples themselves was also a regular occurrence and those living in the south and southwestern Chinese provinces freely crossed the shared borders with Vietnam, Laos and Burma. Further away lay Thailand and India. Over time, war and natural migration have also contributed to the dissemination of various minority crafts and the cross-fertilization of religious and ethnic identities.

Religious beliefs are especially diverse among China's many ethnic minorities and remain widely influential in day-to-day life. Lamaism, a sect of Buddhism, has many followers in regions close to Tibet. Islam can be found in China's northwest provinces and a flood of Protestant

An opulent Dragon Boat is propelled through the water by oarsmen to the beat of drums and gongs in honour of China's first poet, Qu Yuan. A shrine located near the bow honours a deity unique to each boat.

missionaries during the nineteenth century succeeded in making many converts along China's eastern seacoast. Perhaps even more interesting for their effect on regional crafts and religious arts, however, are the minority beliefs involving fetishism, polytheism, totemism and shamanism, which have been arduously maintained in the Dong, Bouyei, Jingpo and Miao communities. Through elaborate rituals played out in secluded temples, minority peoples utilize the traditions of storytelling, music and dance to ensure the continuity of their ancient beliefs. In some polytheistic villages, impressive wooden totems and intricately carved masks play an important role in ceremonial exorcisms that are still accompanied by animal sacrifices.

In many provinces stone totems representing fabled animals and watchful deities are placed along winding rural paths as guardians for those on pilgrimage. Foot bridges are also commonly festooned with stone sculptures, protecting those who

pass as their feet momentarily leave solid earth to cross the abyss beneath them. Many bridge carvings are comprised of the animals of the zodiac and, like China's highly arched moon bridges, which reflect a complementary image in the water beneath to form a perfect circle, the presence of the duodenary figures serves to remind us of the cyclical nature of the universe. Similar references to wholeness and continuity are regularly manifested in abstract folk designs and applied to items as varied as embroidered clothing and carved lacquer pendants.

The celebration of the annual mid-autumn or Moon Festival, held on the fifteenth day of the eighth lunar month, is a time of similar contemplation. During the *Zhongqiu Jie*, as it is known, family and friends gather together to recite poetry and gaze at the moon in wonder and admiration of its perfect beauty. Much of the melancholy poetry written during the Tang era is filled with references to the cyclical

An intricate good luck paper cut featuring a seated woman surrounded by a pair of hens and fish. Hens are believed to drive away evil, while fish traditionally symbolize abundance. Shaanxi Province.

forces of nature, the expansiveness of the universe and the transience of life.

Such traditions imbue each of China's principal festivals, which originated with primitive fertility or funerary rites and are linked to natural phenomena, seasons of planting and periods of harvest. The *Duanwu Jie* or Dragon Boat Festival, held on the fifth day of the fifth moon, corresponds to the summer solstice. It is an important period in Chinese cosmology, since the previous months of growth and maturation, represented by the *yang*, fall into a period of decline and decay as governed by the *yin*. The *Duanwu Jie* grew out of the rhythms of cultivation; peasants finishing the transplanting of rice awaited the summer's nourishing rain. To ensure a wet summer they regularly sought the good will of the dragon god, who ruled over water, rivers and seas. Elaborate ceremonies involving swimming competitions and dragon boat races now mark the event, which is also accompanied by the ceremonial eating of *zongzi*, a glutinous rice dumpling made in honour of the drowned poet, Qu Yuan.

Certainly the most widely celebrated festival during the year and the one for which the greatest number of colourful and symbolic arts and crafts are still produced is the Chinese New Year. Lasting anywhere from three days to two weeks, *Xin Nian* is the traditional period for sweeping away trouble and misfortune. In anticipation of the festivities, local artisans produce an astonishing variety of simple crafts in recognition of the many spirits and gods that have guided and watched over them during the past year. Fresh paper cuts bearing symbolic images and characters of good fortune are pasted on windows and doors, new woodblock prints are hung near the hearth and colourful clay toys are presented to the younger children.

Official recognition of the New Year holiday and the cessation of regular activities has helped to ensure the continuation of many ancient crafts, often overshadowed during other festivals by the hustle and bustle of modern life. The slow erosion of China's traditional culture, which is due in part to new economic pressures, has forced many artisans to reduce or to abandon much of their craft work to keep pace with changing times.

Happily, many Chinese folk traditions still benefit from the enormous insularity of the country and the resistance of its rural people to uncertain change. Ancient celebrations corresponding to the New Year, the sowing of seeds and the harvesting of crops all remain immutable features of village life because they are inextricably tied to the labours themselves. Thus, it is in this context of celebrating the success of their own labours and the passing of the seasons that so many artisans continue to produce their inspired crafts, keeping alive traditions that reaffirm China's unique creative and spiritual origins.

TEXTILES & EMBROIDERY

From the first of the month to the fifteenth,
stitch, oh, stitch the purses

– verse from a Chinese folk song

The textile arts, particularly those of weaving, dyeing and embroidery, play a principal role in the folk arts and crafts of China. The sewing and decoration of clothing not only serves to protect the people from the extremes of the environment, but also assumes important ceremonial and symbolic functions throughout the year. Through colour, form, pattern, weave and stitch, each piece of clothing is imbued with unique characteristics that distinguish and identify the ethnic origin, social stature or religious beliefs of the wearer. Emphasis on familial and ethnic continuity is especially strong in Chinese tradition, and expressive dress, particularly during festival periods, remains one of the predominant means of retaining and honouring the customs of many generations.

The tremendous diversity of China's ethnic minorities, spread across 29 provinces, creates a country rich in exotic hand-sewn costumes and headdresses, which are determined by a combination of geographic conditions, climate, lifestyle and the aesthetic traditions of the region. For people of the north and northwest

An early photo of a woman from the Black Miao minority. Her clothing is typical of the sophisticated weaving, dyeing and embroidery skills developed by the Miao over many centuries. Guizhou Province.

provinces, where the cold can be severe, knee-high leather boots and long fur-lined robes are the standard, while in the south, lighter cotton fabrics forming skirts and *tongqun* ('sarongs') predominate. Historians have come to understand the development and diversification of several of China's ethnic cultures by studying the changes in their apparel. The Miao, for example, who constitute one of China's largest minorities, refer to themselves as *'Hmong'*, which literally translated means 'cotton clothes' people. This choice of name is indicative of the enormous importance cotton cloth has held for the Miao over many centuries. Forced in ancient times to abandon their villages and flee, the Miao decorated their clothing with representations of the principal fauna and flora of their homelands. With time, the original colours and images have been gradually simplified and abstracted, and now function as important reminders of their disparate geographic origins.

The most common rural clothes worn by both men and women well into the twentieth century were the *shan ku*, a two-piece outfit featuring a long side-fastening over-garment (shan) with loose-fitting pants (ku). Shan ku were originally made with a cloth woven of hemp or ramie. This was later replaced by homespun cotton, dyed a deep blue or black and occasionally immersed in ox blood to add a rich reddish cast. Variations of the *shan,* or jacket, continue to be worn today by rural women and its basic construction has been the basis for many traditional styles of minority dress. Long-wearing and practical, the *shan ku* are always amply cut but never excessive, carefully designed to accommodate the body in a variety of daily labours without unnecessary waste of material. In the southwest provinces many minority women still wear a short, side-fastening *shan* with bands of embroidery, contrasting fabric or braiding along the neckline, down the arms, around the cuffs or along the bottom hem. Variations of fasteners may include braided buttons, silver buttons or even old coins. The *shan* is then worn either with loose-fitting cotton pants or with pleated or layered skirts, depending on the people and the region.

Although silk is the textile first and foremost associated with China because of its historical importance in trade with the West, it was the early introduction of cotton cultivation that had the greatest affect on the lives and dress of the average Chinese. Tales of intrigue and adventure along the Silk Road are legion and the trade that the route spawned did indeed allow China to develop a virtual monopoly in silk manufacturing. The growth in silk exports during the Zhou Dynasty in the last millennium BC brought tremendous wealth to the Imperial Court; examples of the luxurious fabric spread through Syria, India and finally Rome, creating unprecedented demand. The methods for its production were carefully guarded secrets and remained so until the fifth century when a Chinese princess is said to have concealed

Early engraving of a pedal-operated silk-reeling apparatus. Filaments from several cocoons are drawn onto a revolving spindle to produce the final silk thread.

A young woman with bound feet works at a treadle loom while an elderly woman spins thread.

several silkworm eggs inside her headdress on her way to marry the King of Khotan. Certainly sericulture eventually spread westward, expanding to the Mediterranean area by the sixth century. Although European silk manufacturing achieved some success, it was never sufficient to satisfy European demand and Chinese silks remained much in vogue.

Prior to the Han Dynasty (206 BC–AD 220), the wearing of fine silks in China was restricted to a very small portion of the population. Imperial orders forbade silk clothing for all but noble families, court officials and others of high standing. Although these rules were subsequently relaxed, the cost of silk was far beyond the reach of the average Chinese, who viewed cotton as a welcome alternative to clothing made of wool or hemp.

Popular legend credits the advances in cotton production to the peasant woman Huang Daopo. Born in the mid-thirteenth century near present-day Shanghai, Huang fled to Hainan Island to escape poverty and an oppressive family life. There she was introduced to the highly advanced cotton cultivation and dyeing techniques of the Li

minority, not yet practised on the mainland. After remaining on Hainan for some thirty years, Huang Daopo returned home to share her knowledge of cotton cultivation with others. With her she carried seeds, a treadle loom and advanced ginning, carding and spinning techniques that accelerated many aspects of cotton processing. These innovations quickly spread to neighbouring provinces, allowing cotton cloth to be made more economically and thus become more affordable for the average person.

As the popularity of cotton cloth continued to spread, China's minority people developed formidable dyeing techniques by applying their knowledge of local flora. In southern China this contributed to a burgeoning textile trade, also fuelled by demand from Southeast Asia and abroad. Urban textile manufacturing was further aided by the arrival of synthetic dyes shortly after their invention in England in 1856. Aniline purple, later called mauveine, became known as *yang lian zi* ('imported lotus purple') and was widely praised for its intense, if garish, colour.

Today, it remains almost exclusively the minority peoples who preserve the traditions of planting and cultivation to assure a steady supply of natural vegetal dyes. The ubiquitous *lancao* ('indigo') in widespread use throughout China is especially popular among China's southern minority peoples, such as the Miao and Bouyei. Although synthetic indigo has been used in China since the early twentieth century, natural indigo remains the preferred choice among many minorities.

Mordant dyes are especially popular for the rich, permanent colours produced when bonding occurs between the fibre and dye compounds. This may result from soluble matter being released naturally by the plant during boiling, as is the case with

tannic acid released during the boiling of sumac or gall nuts, or from the addition of special mordant substances in the preliminary or post-dyeing baths. The most common Chinese mordants are alum and potash, which are obtained by boiling hemp or rice straw. Their use in varying amounts allows a broader range of tonalities to develop among textiles submerged in the same dye.

Reds, pinks and mauves, which constitute the most cherished tones in Chinese folk textiles, are obtained from boiling the wild munjeet plant known as *qiancao (Rubia cordifolia)* or safflower *(Carthamus tinctorus)*. Collected in the winter when they can be pulled easily from the ground with their roots intact, the plants are sun- or hearth-dried and then ground to a powder. Other reds are produced using sappan wood, or the local betel nut, which is also chewed by minority peoples as a mild stimulant, rendering the saliva a startling crimson.

Variations of brown are produced by drying the green outer layers of the walnut *(Juglans regia)*, or acorns from the chestnut oak *(Quercus serrata)*, with a mordant of

iron sulphite. Yellows come from golden thread *(Coptis trifolia)*, which is pressed to obtain its valued juice, or turmeric *(Curcuma longa)* mordanted with potash. Purples, green and blacks are most often prepared as mixtures of the primary colours or achieved through multiple-dye baths. From these simple beginnings, additional colouring and patterning techniques are often employed to embellish further the clothing with the folk motifs of the region.

In Yunnan Province young Bai women continue a long tradition of tie-dyeing, which dates to the Southern Dynasties (AD 265–589). In a time-consuming process, natural homespun is bound with fine threads into small bunches and knots. Once the fabric is coloured, the threads are removed to reveal a complex pattern of flower and starburst designs. Throughout China's southern provinces many beautiful textiles also continue to be made by *laran*, or batik printing. By this method a resist agent, such as bean paste, lime mortar or wax, is directly applied to the untreated fabric in order to block contact with the future dye. One of the earliest methods of transferring a *laran* design to cloth involved

Two examples of blue and white starch-resist stencil-dyed fabrics. (left) *Flower and gourd motif from Jiangsu Province.* (right) *Butterfly pattern from Zhejiang Province.*

the technique of wax rubbing. As sections of cloth were placed over large bronze drums decorated with relief patterns, a block of wax was rubbed over the fabric surface, recording the drum design beneath. The fabric was then dyed and left to dry until a final boiling in clear water removed all traces of the wax resist. The resulting design copied that of the ceremonial drum and was a fitting counterpart when used in festival or ceremonial attire.

Today, intricate *laran* patterns are most commonly produced using stencilling techniques. In this process decorative motifs are cut out of heavy-gauge paper or thin wood sheets. In the case of wood stencils, which predate the use of paper, the wax was poured directly into the carved holes and left to harden. Paper stencils, while less durable, are easier to cut and allow for the creation of more inventive, spontaneous and flowing designs. Once the stencil is affixed to the fabric, molten wax is simply brushed across the perforated surface, leaving trace designs on the fabric. In the case of both wood and paper stencils, the design can be easily repeated by simply moving the stencil and continuing in the same manner. When printing is required on both sides, the fabric is clamped between a pair of identical stencils and the resist applied uniformly to both sides.

The popularity of stencilled dye-resist fabric is evidenced by the many fine designs available today. Bolts of beautiful indigo blue and white printed cotton may be found throughout China and local markets near *laran* communities take special pride in offering their own regional motifs. The simplest of *laran* designs are those of repeated geometric diamond and square motifs. Stylized floral patterns are also common and are frequently made into skirts, aprons, scarves and shoulder bags.

Other thematic *laran* prints include abstract representations of animals, including bats, dragons and phoenix, which are printed as single panels depicting popular folk tales, such as 'The magpie in the plum tree' or 'Dragon and phoenix playing with a peony'. Each theme holds special significance and often determines how that design will be used or to whom it might be given. Many individual *laran* panels become the central image for a quilt cover, or serve as *baofu*, which are decorative cloths used for wrapping and carrying packages.

An important method of fabric decoration in widespread practice in Miao villages is *ladao*, or the 'wax knife' technique, which involves the drawing of elaborate designs by hand. The resulting blue and white textiles are highly prized among collectors. In contrast with basic dye-resist fabrics, whose use is generally decided after the dyeing is complete, *ladao* is begun with a specific idea and purpose, such as a headband, waistband or clothing panel design. The knife consists of a polished bamboo stick, which is fitted with a small brass reservoir. Molten wax from the reservoir is channelled to a finely crafted blade or stylus, creating a liquid pen with which to draw on the natural homespun. As many as ten different pens, with varying size nibs, may be used to create a single design. When the wax cools, tiny fissures and cracks appear; these allow the colour to spread in hairlike webs as the fabric is submerged in the dye bath. After the fabric is boiled to remove the original wax, the process is easily repeated through a succession of darker dyes, creating complex multi-coloured layers of tremendous richness and dimension.

Today, some of the most representative wax-resist works of the Miao minority come from Daizai and Huangping in Guizhou Province. Textiles from Daizai feature large surface areas and broad simplified designs inspired by ancient motifs. The artisans of Huangping specialize in concise tightly grouped geometric forms integrating plant and animal references. Similar styles are also produced by the Bouyei, who live close to the Miao in south-central Guizhou Province. They are also highly skilled in the production of beautiful batik, which has been an integral part of both daily and ceremonial attire for centuries. Bouyei women traditionally wear a long embroidered coat, with inset arm panels of fine blue and white resist designs, over a long pleated batik skirt. Batik was recognized by the central government as an important traditional craft in the 1950s, and a factory was built at Anshun in Guizhou Province to merge modern technology with traditional Bouyei techniques. As a result, batik has become the Bouyei's most well-known handicraft. The designs produced today in Anshun have suffered from a slow commercialization, but vivid dye work is still available in smaller neighbouring communities. The widespread acceptance and popularity of Anshun-style textiles is an encouraging sign for folk textiles and their availability in cities across China has assured the continuation of the artisanal dye-resist tradition.

Throughout China's long textile history, the arts of weaving and dyeing have been complemented by the use of fanciful *xiuhua* (embroidery). The earliest surviving records are those of chain-stitched impressions found on clay vessels of the Western Zhou Dynasty (c. 1050–771 BC) discovered in Shaanxi Province. Fragments of cloth bearing ornamental chain-stitch designs, which have been unearthed in tombs in Henan Province dating from the early Spring and Autumn period (770–475 BC), parallel the growth in popularity of multicoloured brocade. However, the demand for embroidery far outshone that of woven cloth; complex stitchery was more certain to bring the admiration of others. By the Warring States period (475–421 BC), popular embroidery designs included plants, flowers, birds, phoenix and tigers. In addition to their aesthetic or decorative functions, the use of such auspicious symbols was also highly regarded for its protective properties against calamity, sickness and misfortune. The sun, moon and stars each represented the shedding of light or knowledge; mountains evoked solidity and permanence; dragons were equated with male vigour and fertility; wine vessels suggested filial piety and water plants served as symbols for purity.

Embroidery examples dating to the Western Han Dynasty (206 BC–AD 9) have also been uncovered along the Silk Road, indicating an early interest in the decoration of common objects and non-ceremonial clothing. These finds include embroidered mirror and make-up cases, and variations of *wangxiu* ('net embroidery'), which were probably intended as trim pieces for jackets or robes. However, the technique of *suozeng* (chain-stitch), in its many variations (open ring, closed ring, braid, loop, daisy and fly stitch), constituted the principal embroidery method for symbolic motifs well through the end of the Eastern Han Dynasty (AD 25–220).

During the Northern and Southern Dynasties (AD 265–581) and extending into the Tang Dynasty (AD 618–906), a growing interest in Buddhist imagery saw the introduction of the satin-stitch to render better the subtleties of natural forms. Examples from this period often depict Sakayamuni standing amid mountain peaks flanked by an entourage of smaller Buddhas and lions. These scenes reflect a highly developed training and suggest that the embroiderers may also have had extensive experience as painters. The introduction of the layered short stitch,

which falls within the satin-stitch category, was instrumental in creating sophisticated shading techniques and graduated tones. The rise in popularity of the satin-stitch significantly increased the consumption of embroidery thread in comparison to the earlier, more conservative stitches. Nevertheless, its popular acceptance may be attributed to major aesthetic and technical advances in the refinement of embroidery materials, as well as a marked increase in the prosperity of the period. Once practised with an economy of materials and costs, embroidery had now become a mark of social stature for which one paid increasingly large sums in order to wear the finest work available.

This demand for exceptional embroidery provided many opportunities for girls from poor families to supplement their family income, a practice which continues to this day. However, this was certainly not the sole source for finely embroidered goods. Before the advent of factory-made cloth even the daughters of wealthy families were taught the arts of weaving, dyeing and embroidery as a way of increasing the young woman's dowry. Known as 'boudoir embroidery', such pieces consisted primarily of quilt covers, pillowcases and other articles to be used in establishing a new household. The quality of a young woman's work, regardless of her origins, was never treated lightly and would have a direct affect on her future. For hundreds of years Chinese women were chosen for marriage based on the sophistication and mastery of their embroidery skills rather than their beauty, for it was thought that only through the complexities of a woman's stitchery could one catch a glimpse of her true inner nature.

During the Ming Dynasty (AD 1368–1644) couture embroidery was transformed into an art of significant scale and began to attract serious interest from abroad. Many

Typical cross-stitch embroidery patterns from Shaanxi Province: geometric butterflies, figures and wheat. This type of embroidery is often used for belt sashes, shoulder bags and household trims.

fine examples of embroidered Chinese robes *(changpao)* were purchased during this period by Portuguese and Spanish traders for the European market. As a consequence of the introduction of Chinese textiles to the West and the huge demand it triggered, the cost of such handicraft work skyrocketed to such a level that silver, newly obtained from Spanish conquests in Latin America, became the *de facto* currency in the trade with China.

Imperial appreciation for elaborate couture embroidery may be traced to the ancient *Book of Documents,* in which the Emperor Shun requests of his young successor Yu: 'I wish to see the signs of the ancients; the sun, moon, stars, mountains, dragons, and the flowery fowl, together with temple vessels, aquatic grasses, fire, rice, and other embroidered decorations, emblazoned on your garments in all the five colours.'

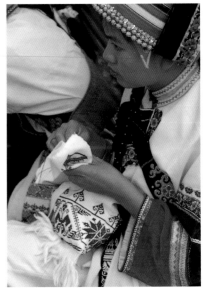

(Clockwise from upper left) *Embroidered aprons and shoulder bags at a rural market in Shilin, Yunnan Province; Yi minority girl from Yunnan Province engaged in intricate cross-stitch; Bai minority woman selling an assortment of embroidered hats, vests and purses in Dali, Yunnan Province; richly embroidered bei er bu, or baby-carrier, bearing auspicious symbols. Shilin, Yunnan Province.*

His suggested use of the 'five colours' is a reference to an elemental order of natural forces thought to govern the world. Yellow represents the earth; azure symbolizes wood; white suggests metal; red represents fire; and black corresponds to water. These forces work together in a continuous cycle presiding over periods of creation and destruction, rebirth and decay. In this elemental hierarchy wood reigns over earth; metal prevails over wood; fire triumphs over metal; water douses fire; and earth covers water. Thus the five colours, when used together in embroidery, are referred to as the 'threads of life' and serve to protect the wearer from malicious forces.

Symbolic and decorative embroidery also play important roles among China's minority cultures. *Tiaohua* ('cross-stitch embroidery') is a traditional Miao technique practised over a thousand years. It is characterized by the white thread that is cross-stitched from the back on black homespun cloth. The pattern or image is never predetermined but evolves as the embroiderer works, avoiding any glance at the finished side. This method, as well as standard embroidery techniques, is generally introduced to girls at the age of eight or nine years. They practise in groups in preparation for the sewing of complicated festival *beipai* ('back plates'). These rectangular pieces are joined with other panels to form a decorative vestment that slips over the head. Such finely detailed clothing can take over a year to produce and is the ultimate test of a girl's embroidery skill. The design often becomes so dense and complicated as to take on a relief quality and a final weight of more than four or five times that of the original cloth. During festival periods, several elaborately embroidered layers of clothing, including skirts, jackets and vests of differing lengths, are worn together in a show of talent.

In Yunnan Province and in the northern Miao communities of Guizhou, elaborate waistbands of birds, flowers and fish are embroidered by the young women in preparation for a special event known as the 'Stepping over flower mountains' festival at the beginning of May. There they are tied to the waist of the young man of their choice as an engagement offering. If accepted, the waistband becomes a token of fidelity and devotion; it will be worn again on the couple's wedding day.

By the age of fifteen or sixteen, Miao girls begin what is known as *mixiu* ('secret embroidery'). Consisting of elaborately decorated children's hats, shoes, clothing and quilts, it is done alone in a girl's spare time and is carefully wrapped and hidden as the work progresses. By the time a girl is ready for marriage, she may have completed as many as fifteen hats, twenty sets of clothes, ten pairs of shoes and eight quilts. When everything is complete the embroidery is once again carefully

wrapped, with the same items together, and given to the mother for safekeeping; it is only brought out for all to see when presented to the girl's first baby at the age of one month. To aid in the celebration, the husband's family prepares an extravagant banquet and the embroidered clothing is laid out on a table to be admired by the guests, who are expected to compliment the new mother on her skilful labours.

Such devotion to the sewing of symbolic garments does not end with the birth of the child. Patchwork and appliqué baby-carriers, with painstakingly embroidered designs, are still commonly used today. Similar to a modern knapsack, they consist of a padded fabric panel with shoulder and waist straps that tie in the front, allowing the baby to be carried on the mother's back in complete security and comfort as she continues her daily activities. Images of

auspicious animals and bold geometric patterns dominate the central panel, with strings of beads, tiny bells, metal studs or brilliant sequins added for decoration.

To protect their clothing beneath, rural women of all ages continue to wear lightweight embroidered aprons *(weiqun)* regardless of their work. Some versions feature an additional embroidered flap disguising a small pocket for money or other daily necessities. When travelling away from home, it is customary for minority women to carry brightly embroidered shoulder bags or waist purses. They are used to hold simple foods to be eaten during the journey, tobacco, or possibly areca, which is chewed as a digestive. The Hani, Bai and Jingpo are especially well known for their elaborate bags, often integrating old coins, colourful beads, swinging tassels and even shells.

Blue and white resist-printed cottons. (left) *Diamond flower motif from Ansun, Guizhou Province.* (right) *Butterfly and phoenix motif from Kunming, Yunnan Province.*

Perhaps the most whimsical and original examples of folk embroidery are found on children's clothing and handmade toys. In rural villages, which once lacked basic medical care and where infant mortality was high, superstition assumed an important role in the protection of children. In the Han culture the maternal grandmother traditionally presented her grandson with decorative hats, collars, vests and shoes, all bearing auspicious symbols in appliqué and embroidery, designed to ward off roaming spirits which might cause harm to the defenceless child. Many hats and shoes are made in the likeness of dogs or pigs, which – when seen by spirits – fool them into thinking that the child is only a common animal and not worth harming. Lotus flower and pomegranate motifs are frequent decorations, for these fruits are known for their abundant seeds and represent an implicit wish for further male offspring. The cosmological symbols *yin* and *yang* are frequent embellishments, as are the Buddhist swastika and the character *wan*, which both represent longevity.

Tigers have always been the preferred theme for a variety of stuffed animals, hats, pillows and shoes, so that by day or night the child would never go unprotected. Their appearance, sewn atop a child's hat, was certain to scare away any lingering ghosts and ensure that the child would grow up as strong and fearless as the animal itself. The sewing of Chinese characters onto clothing, using playful homonyms, remains a widespread practice. The character *hu*, meaning 'tiger', may also sound like the word for 'wealth' and its use on a garment is believed to assure the child of a prosperous future. The character *fu*, meaning 'bat', also sounds like 'luck'. Thus, the desire for luck is often represented symbolically by its visual counterpart. Whether on a pillow or hat,

Tiger paper cut bearing the character wang *for 'king'. The tiger is considered the king of animals and his appearance on clothing protects a child from harm.*

the forehead of a cloth tiger usually bears the character *wang*, meaning 'king', in reference to the king of the animals. Elaborately sewn tiger shoes are also popular gifts given to a young child and it is believed that the additional set of embroidered eyes will help the young child to see more clearly where he is walking.

Most cloth crafts usually feature some use of appliqué, which is widely practised in conjunction with folk embroidery. The technique is especially popular in Shaanxi Province, where scraps of appliqué fabric are combined with geometric patchwork quilting to create brightly coloured children's vests and purses bearing the five poisons known as *wu du*. Snakes, centipedes, scorpions, lizards and toads are each thought to be poisonous and bring bad luck to the unprotected. As a precaution, they are often stitched in relief or sewn in appliqué on vests and purses so that no harm will come to the wearer.

Appliqué is also used to decorate fragrant sachets that are given to young and old during *Duanwu Jie* or Dragon Boat Festival. Filled with various medicinal herbs and spices to ward off disease, the sachets

are hung in the home or pinned to clothes for the duration of the festival, which corresponds to the time when people believe most diseases are likely to strike. At the end of the festival, the sachet is thrown into the river or abandoned along the road to avoid bringing disease into the home.

Economical and durable, amusing appliqué toys have also been crafted in Shaanxi Province for many centuries. Free of rules or practical constraints, the miniature birds and free-standing animals sewn in the rural homes near Xian are limited only by the imaginations of their makers. Many are symbols for happiness or prosperity, or are inspired by ancient folktales. Suspended over a child's crib, marvellous swimming fish made from tiny scraps of cloth swim effortlessly in the evening breeze, all the while casting their favour on the sleeping child for an abundant or plentiful life. A pair of butterflies – renowned symbols for longevity – turn gracefully in a circle from a fine thread tied to an overhead beam. Well-known animals from the popular folktale, *Journey to the West*, and composite creatures such as the benevolent *qiling*, continue to enthral Chinese children as they have for centuries. No two are ever exactly alike, for each is made with a unique combination of fabric scraps, which have been carefully tucked away in a basket for just this purpose. Sewing in groups, the village women trade stories of their children and grandchildren with the same ease that they exchange pieces of cloth, yarn and sequins needed to complete their simple toys. In some instances, word of a woman's exceptional sewing and appliqué skills travels far beyond the confines of her immediate community, bringing her the satisfaction of knowing that distant villages have learned of her special devotion and love for a newborn child.

JEWELRY & ADORNMENT

*May your bellows forever glow red with brilliant fire
and the sounds from your silver hammer
shake the beams of every household by day and night*

– Dai minority folk song from Xishuangbanna, Yunnan

The adornment of the human body with precious stones and metals is one of the most widespread and celebrated customs on earth. In China, gold, silver and jade have long been fashioned into jewelry and worn by even the most humble of rural families. Rings and necklaces, passed from generation to generation, are presented to a bride by her family at marriage, maintaining an important ancestral bond. Countless stories have been told of the misery and suffering a family might endure before resorting to the final humiliation of selling such an heirloom. For those who could purchase new jewelry it was often done with the belief that precious metals and stones bore curative or protective properties, a belief that remains largely intact today.

One of the earliest stones thought to be imbued with mystical powers is *lüsong shi* or turquoise, which was cherished in China, Mongolia and Tibet for its ability to protect the wearer from evil. Hubei Province has provided much of the pale blue stone, which has been crafted and formed into jewelry for centuries. Its earliest uses were as decorative inlays on bronze vessels and on primitive bone rings,

found in tombs dating to the ancient Dawenkou culture (*c.* 4300–2400 BC). Belief in its power was once so strong that it was even used as a powdered ingredient in traditional medicines.

The translucent glow of amber also developed an early mystical following, based on its deep golden colour. Known as *hupo* ('tiger soul'), amber was believed to be the dead animal's spirit, which had buried itself deep in the earth. Formed from fossilized pine resin subjected to long periods of intense pressure and high temperatures, amber often bears the markings of ancient insects or flora trapped in the slowly hardening substance.

References to amber in the ancient geographic work, *Classic of Mountains and Seas,* note its magical power to protect the wearer from illness and pain. In the *Lun Heng,* an ancient text that defined relationships between spiritual and physical bodies, the author Wang Chong delighted in his discovery of its magical ability to attract and hold small particles on its surface, a reference to the static electricity created when amber is rubbed. His public demonstrations of its amazing

magnetic properties never failed to draw large crowds, engendering cries of amazement and awe.

Although most Chinese amber is found in Yunnan Province near the Burmese border, examples of ancient jewelry bearing amber, agate and rock crystal beads have been uncovered in tombs throughout the country. Han Dynasty tombs discovered in Guangdong and Guangxi Provinces, in particular, have yielded significant amounts of amber jewelry, suggestive of its tremendous popularity in ceremony and trade during this period. Indeed, it is said that the Western Han Empress, Chao Feiyen, regularly slept on a solid amber pillow, benefiting from its protective properties and enamoured by the gentle fragrance that it emitted when warm.

Although amber is not widely used today in artisanal jewelry, married women of the Nu minority in Yunnan's Bijiang and Fugong Counties are fond of wearing coral ornaments in their hair and ears, as well as other exotic jewelry in agate, shell and glass. Of the many varieties of coral that exist, the Chinese refer to 'Noble Coral' as the only one suitable for jewelry. Its colour ranges from white, pink, red and blue to purple and even black. With its fine veins and glossy surface, coral was considered one of the seven Buddhist treasures. Although documents such as the *Tien Chu Kuo Chuan (History of the Southern Dynasty)* mention the importation of coral from the Roman Empire, significant quantities are also found off the coasts of Taiwan and Japan. Coral is relatively soft and easily engraved, though its brittle nature makes intricate work a delicate and time-consuming task. Coral composites and imitations also abound. Inexpensive horn and bone substitutes are often dyed and then heat-treated to produce the appearance of more expensive coral.

The Bai minority residing in Yunnan Province has excelled in the lapidary arts for centuries, producing both sacred and profane carvings in many genres. The Bai preference for marble is connected to the discovery of large deposits around Mount Diancang, overlooking Lake Erhai. The white stone is typically streaked with veins of brilliant red, green and milky yellow, and is used to fashion marble jewelry and decorative objects for sale in nearby Dali. The ancient practice of carving marble and other hard stones for use in jewelry is also exemplified by the exquisite stone bracelets and neck ornaments which originate in the hills surrounding Mount Lishan, east of Xian in Shaanxi Province. Richly grained in sepia, grey, rust and ochre, the stone adornments are simply carved, reflecting the perfect circularity that characterized China's earliest amuletic jewelry.

Certainly no stone has held such long-standing symbolic importance, been more valued or so closely associated with a culture than jade. Throughout history jade has been held in reverence at every level of Chinese society. It is considered to be the most beautiful of all stones and to this day

is regularly used as a metaphor for virtue, strength and superiority. Its early refinement during China's Neolithic period made jade the choice for personal jewelry over that of precious metal. In the Eastern Han document *Shuo Wen*, Xu Shen explains its noble character: 'Jade, as a stone, has five virtues. Its glossiness and warmth is like benevolence. Because inside and outside it is the same, so that knowing the outside, one knows the inside, this may be likened to righteousness. Its far-reaching sound (when struck) may be heard from afar, like wisdom. It is not easily bent, but can be broken, which may be likened to courage. Jade can be sharpened, but not to the point where it can injure people; this quality is like self-regulation or restraint.'

By tradition, a family was thought fortunate to bear a son and in recognition of this blessing often presented male progeny with a piece of jade. In turn it was common to receive the congratulations of friends and neighbours for having acquired 'a fine piece of jade', meaning a male child. In some cases the donning of such symbolic

Carved jade fish pendants: early symbols of abundance. Beijing, Hebei Province.

jewelry was assisted by a priest or shaman, who would chant a powerful incantation to assist the jade in warding off evil spirits capable of bringing serious illness or premature death to a newborn child.

Archaeological finds from as early as the Neolithic period suggest that artisans were willing to travel great distances to collect this magical stone, which was then cut and polished into a variety of hair ornaments, rings and amulets. During the Eastern Zhou and Han Dynasties, ornamental neck pendants and belts were carved in jade in the belief that they would protect the body from injury. Elaborate funerary suits of small jade plaques, linked with gold threads, have also been unearthed in the Western Han tombs of Prince Liu Sheng and his wife, Dou Wan, in Mancheng, Hebei Province. These sumptuous adornments indicate the growing Chinese preoccupation with immortality and the belief that jade would preserve the body after death, serving the departing soul in its voyage to the afterlife.

In ancient China the term 'jade' was originally used to embrace several types of hard stones, ranging in colour from green-grey to brown and black. Today jade refers most commonly either to nephrite, which is almost almost exclusively limited to finds in Xinjiang Province, or to jadeite, which comes from China's southwest border regions, a source unknown prior to the eighteenth century. Jade's great importance in ancient ritual and later as a cherished collectible among scholar-officials has assured it a high place in the hierarchy of Chinese art, surpassing precious metals and other stones, which were never imbued with the same historical or spiritual significance.

As a result of this intense preoccupation with jade, few examples of jewelry in precious metal are known prior to the Han Dynasty, although metal casting was

Silver chest ornaments as worn by Jingpo women during the traditional Munao festival of music and dance, which is held on the fifteenth day of the first lunar month.

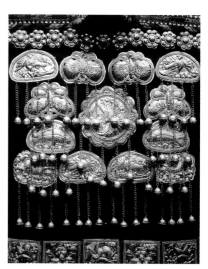

Silver repoussé clothing ornaments decorated with flower, bird, butterfly and fish motifs and strung with rows of tiny bells. Miao minority, Guizhou Province.

practised from an early date. Techniques for the casting of iron were developed in China by the sixth century BC, a skill only acquired in Europe during the late Middle Ages. By the Shang and Zhou eras, cast bronze reliquary vessels reached their peak of sophistication, using elaborate piece-mould construction methods. Other precious metals were probably worked in the same manner. During the Warring States period, the lost wax method of cast-ing and soldering was introduced to the art of metalsmithing, while the Han Dynasty saw the introduction of granulation, a technique highly developed in Etruscan goldsmithing. This method presumably arrived from the Mediterranean by way of India, where it was used in the final centuries BC. Each of these individual innovations had a fundamental impact on the development and refinement of regional jewelry-making.

The earliest use of gold, silver and gilt bronze jewelry is thought to have been introduced by Chinese minority cultures during the Southern Dynasties as a result of contacts with nomadic peoples along the northern and northwestern border areas. Such works, intended as personal ornaments and harness decorations, were crafted in animal shapes. A cast silver belt buckle, found in the Ordos desert region along the northern reaches of the Yellow River, is suggestive of a crouching pony or mule. Belt hooks in precious metals were also common from an early period and led to the use of silver belt plaques, embossed with tiger, phoenix and palmette designs, during the Sui period (AD 589–618). Among the non-minority population the use of gold adornment was largely restricted to embroidery and appliqué designs, coming into broader acceptance only during the Han Dynasty.

Economic and cultural exchanges between China and other parts of Asia reached new heights during the Tang Dynasty (AD 618–906) and brought a major influx of foreign tastes that greatly affected the decorative arts. Elaborate silver vessels from the Near East and Central Asia made their way overland via traders on the Silk Road, thus fuelling a demand for similar items for which there was little precedent. As objects made their way east, visual motifs from Scythian, Byzantine and Persian cultures were each assimilated and transformed to suit Chinese tastes, eventually finding their way into jewelry designs. The result was a preponderance of leaf and scrolling flower patterns, using the techniques of chasing, whereby the metal surface is hammered or engraved with a series of small chisels and punches.

With the new developments in the decorative arts, the metalsmiths of the Tang period made a gradual transition from ornamental casting to the working of sheet metal and wire filament. This change revolutionized the art of jewelry-making and allowed artisans to produce ever larger designs at greatly reduced weights. As a result, late Tang silversmiths produced magnificent diadems and hairpins in complex wire filigree. It was customary for prosperous women of the Tang era to own several gold or silver gilt hairpins, often with decorated and jeweled edges that shone brightly when tucked into their dark hair just above the forehead. Elaborate combs were also very much in vogue, with fine graduated teeth cut from bamboo or bone and banded with raised silver floral designs. Also fashionable were hammered gold bracelets, gracefully tapering to fine coiled wire ends. Most were decorated with mythical animals and scroll patterns, designs which remain practically unchanged in the minority jewelry produced today.

For many minority people, who traversed a wide geographic area in search of a stable and secure environment over several centuries, jewelry provided a form of identification and cultural continuity. Among the Hmong people of northern Thailand, who are related to the Miao of southwestern China, near identical jewelry patterns exist despite the geographic separation of the two peoples. A long history of travel and trade between these communities has ensured the spread of metalsmithing techniques and styles, often obscuring their true technical and aesthetic origins.

Perhaps as a consequence of this cross-fertilization, it is in Yunnan and Guizhou Provinces that the richest and most varied selection of minority jewelry styles can still be seen. The proximity to Vietnam, Laos and Burma has allowed the region greater exposure to outside materials, techniques and aesthetic influences. In addition, Yunnan is home to a third of China's fifty-five minorities and in this sense is a land of living ethnic traditions.

Most minority jewelry is crafted by specialized artisans working in silver-smithing villages. Their skills have been handed down over many generations and they are well versed in the visual traditions of their ancient cultures. Each family has a standard repertoire of the ring, bracelet and necklace designs that have come to characterize their cultural sub-group. The Miao people, who have perhaps the most turbulent history of minority migration in China, are divided into five such sub-groups, each defined by variations of clothing, jewelry, dialect and general living habits. Miao metalsmiths are therefore responsible for safeguarding the important patterns and motifs that have come to define their distinct social unit and its historical traditions.

From time to time these artisans are summoned to produce a special piece of jewelry. This may be a request to copy a lost heirloom or repair a cherished piece inadvertently damaged. Villagers often request the creation of new jewelry conceived for a particular member of the family. A girl nearing the age of courtship might be given jewelry imbued with special powers to protect her and bring her luck as she travels beyond her familiar home. Belief in the amuletic power of the jewelry is accepted without question. These ancient convictions are an acknowledgment of the supreme powers of the silversmiths and, most importantly, the magical properties of their metals. Many of the symbolic associations granted to metal are an outgrowth of their natural physical properties. Iron, for example, symbolized great strength and righteousness; figures cast in the metal were once tossed into rivers and lakes to repel water dragons, who feared its force.

Hundreds of years of evolution and refinement have seen the importance of iron diminish in favour of silver, which was much admired for its durability and resistance to surface deterioration.

Unfortunately, the cost of silver today places it beyond the means of many minority peoples, who lead sparse agrarian lives. For this reason, other metals and alloys are now regularly substituted in designs where silver once reigned. *Baitong* ('white copper') is a prevalent jewelry material that gives the appearance of silver and is often sold as such to unwary buyers. *Baitong* is actually an alloy composed of white copper blended with up to fifty per cent nickel. Other copper alloy variations may include manganese, or even iron. Although the use of *baitong* has risen significantly over the past several decades in jewelry destined for daily wear and the tourist trade, traditional and ceremonial jewelry is still crafted in silver. The relative sanctity of ritual jewelry, however, assures its scarcity on the open market. By contrast, varying grades of personal jewelry can still be purchased from itinerant silversmiths, who tour the village markets and often approach the foreign visitor.

Much of the minority jewelry made today begins as molten metal, which is poured into thin strips and then hammered into basic forms or stretched into metal thread for *xihuo* ('delicate work') or *xihua chao* ('delicate flower weaving'). Bracelets are perhaps the most popular form of daily jewelry among minority women. Most are made by braiding or hammering techniques. Braided styles use silver or other metal filaments, which are interwoven to create flexible bands of varying sizes. By this method the craftsman can also introduce subtle changes in the twisting and grouping of the filaments, as well as filament size, resulting in delicate variations of pattern and weave. Most are left as open cuffs, with the wire ends capped or soldered. The hammering of flat braided sections creates wide, smooth-surfaced bracelets, which may still bear subtle traces of the original woven pattern.

Many bracelets originating with sheet metal are decorated by the ancient methods of chasing and repoussé. The latter, like chasing, involves the hammering of designs into the surface using small punches and forms. Many ornamental bracelets are begun by tracing a rough pattern in ink on the reverse. The pattern can then be hammered out in the repoussé method with a greater regularity of features that can be duplicated many times. Fine surface chasing then increases and defines the heavy relief, after which the bracelets are rolled, soldered and polished to produce stunning designs. The fact that most are hollow leaves them comfortably lightweight, making it easy for women to wear several at a time. Now and then a metal bead is inserted into the cavity to produce a long rolling rattle.

Inherent in much minority jewelry and clothing is the aspect of movement and sound. Bells are especially popular and have a long, diverse history both in Buddhist ceremony and in earlier primitive Chinese folklore. At one time ceremonial bells were sanctified with the blood of sacrificial animals to aid the incantatory powers of the shaman. Today they are still viewed by many as a general talisman against evil. Tales abound of bells eerily possessed with their own spirit, which sent them flying through the air to the exact place where they were to be hung. These peculiar powers are recognized by Jingpo women, who live in the mountains of Yunnan. Wearing as many as six or seven silver neck chains, which are thickly hung with sequins and tiny silver bells, the women freely traverse the dense forests and bamboo groves, knowing that the bells will deliver them to their destination unharmed. As the women walk, the elaborate chains jingle merrily, warning unsuspecting ghosts of their imminent

Three examples of scrolling flower designs from stone epitaphs and reliquaries of the Tang Dynasty, which had a direct influence on the ornamentation of bracelets and lockets. Shaanxi and Gansu Provinces.

approach and thus avoiding any chance of an unwanted encounter.

A characteristic feature of Hani dress is the cylindrically shaped hat worn by the women, which is constructed of coarse deep blue or black homespun cloth and ringed with silver studs. From the brim are hung small silver balls on tiny chains which swing lyrically across the forehead. The rhythmic nature of Hani clothing decoration is further accentuated by the pinning of small silver amulets to the chest. These charms, suspended on fine chains, include miniature scissors, combs and needle boxes, each of which carry powerful symbolic powers to ward of evil. Scissors are one of the most commonly used precautionary charms in China and are believed to 'cut off' harmful contact with malevolent influences.

The decoration of neck chains with silver lockets and needle boxes is also a prevalent feature among traditional Chinese jewelry of all origins. The fine art of embroidery

occupies many idle hours and the delicately crafted boxes and cylinders provide a practical solution for storing the delicate needles for future work. At many times during the year sewing and needlework are actually forbidden. This is the case during the first five days of the New Year when it was said that an active needle might pierce the eye of the Buddha, as well as on the third day of the month, when engaging in embroidery would supposedly make a woman a widow.

Large wire rings, characterized by those of the Miao, have also been a regular feature of women's neckwear for centuries and may be worn several at a time. Neck rings are found in many shapes, from thin wire hoops to flat-hammered collars. Many incorporate sliding bands to expand and contract as they are placed over the head. Neckbands often feature chased panel designs bearing magical animals, or support a row of silver bells or ornamental seeds.

Pair of copper-plated bracelets for a young girl, each with three stamped bells adorned with stylized plum flower designs. Yunnan Province. l.8 cm

Tiny metallic seeds are a regular feature adorning much Chinese jewelry. The word for seed *(zi)* is phonetically similar to that of child or son. Thus the abundant use of decorative seeds is widely recognized as a wish for fertility and progeny. The fish is another popular charm adorning neck chains and lockets. Its phonetic similarity with abundance means that it is often used to invoke great wealth. Used in conjunction with a child, it becomes an auspicious wish for success and high rank.

Children's jewelry remains widespread in China's rural provinces. Neck rings and hoop bracelets hung with miniature bells serve the double function of scaring away lingering spirits while allowing the mother to keep track of the wandering child. For many Hakka people, who live with their children on boats around the southern city of Guangzhou, the ringing of infant jewelry becomes a regular feature of their water-bound lives. Sudden silences alert them to the possibility of a child accidentally swept overboard.

Concern for the health and well-being of offspring stems from ancient Chinese legends which portray mischievous spirits as forever looming in wait to steal an unsuspecting child. These myths grew out of a need to justify and explain infant deaths in remote areas where child mortality was high. For this reason, many families adorned a child with special bracelets or necklaces bearing auspicious inscriptions or images. Such was the gift of a silver padlock, which when hung from a young child's neck symbolically 'locked' him to the earth and protected him from evil. Padlock necklaces are still worn by small boys in many parts of China and are usually engraved along the sides with characters wishing 'long life' or 'a hundred generations of prosperity' as additional protection from harm.

Amulets in silver, or *baitong,* frequently adorn the hats of young children. The most popular charms are those of the Eight Immortals or rows of laughing Buddhas, which are said to alleviate misery and unhappiness. They are all carefully pounded or stamped from thin sheets of metal and stitched across the brow of lovingly embroidered tiger hats. The Eight Immortals ('Ba xian') are guardian figures representing virtue and the quest for eternity. Each carries an identifying object related to his role on earth, such as a staff, flute, lotus flower, gourd or basket of fruit. They are often positioned flanking a larger central amulet of Shou Xing, the God of Longevity. Shou Xing is one of the most endearing and identifiable figures in Chinese folklore, known for his bald, elongated forehead and long flowing white beard. In one hand he carries a cane of knotty bent wood and in the other a peach, the symbol of longevity. The mythical *qiling* is certainly the symbol most associated with children, through its ability to impart great wisdom. Composed of a dragon's head, a scaly body, the hooves of an ox and a lion's tail, it is often modelled with a young boy riding on its back. The special concern given to protecting and nurturing the development of children reflects the continual hope that they will rise above their parents to positions of greater wealth and authority. In a country where primogeniture was non-existent and every child had to succeed on his own merit, each family sought to provide all of the protection and security within their means in an attempt to discredit the popular belief: 'from peasant to peasant in seven generations'.

LACQUER

*Sidewalk shops containing ivory curios and sandalwood fans line the street.
Each may be seen in the process of manufacture. There are shops for
brassware, pewter, silks and porcelains…but the lacquer, ooh the lacquer!
It is amongst the finest! Red, gold and black lacquered boxes. Treasure
chests of the orient!*

– Notes from R.M. Prescot, *Voyage to China*, 1912

From cinnabar-coloured bracelets to folding coromandel screens, the delicate art of lacquer brings to mind an exotic and ancient world rich in wood scents and oils, pigments and polish. Lacquer is a word that immediately evokes a mystical picture of the Orient, with its carefully guarded formulas, ramshackle workshops and greying artisans. Today, nothing could be further from the truth. Far from being rare and expensive commodities, lacquered goods ranging from teapots to pendants are found in even the most modest of Chinese homes. The workshops are brightly lit and airy, and the greying men have been replaced by efficient teams of women artisans, who chat cheerily among themselves as they sand and polish stacks of decorative plates, bowls and boxes. In recent years Chinese lacquerwork has moved far beyond that of respected handicraft, it has become an artistic industry of national pride.

The development of this distinctly Chinese style of decoration may be traced to the Neolithic site of Hemudu in Zhejiang Province (*c.* 5000–3000 BC), where the sap of the lac or sumac tree (*Rhus verniciflua*) was first distilled to form a natural polymer, then applied to woven baskets and containers to make them water- and bug-resistant. Subsequent discoveries led to the addition of natural pigments, such as cinnabar (mercuric sulphide) and carbon black, to create the famous vermilion and black colours, further expanding lacquer's decorative possibilities. Historical records suggest that the use of lacquer decoration developed slowly, for fear that excessive embellishment would draw attention to the significant outlay of time, talent and material it required to make what were still essentially utilitarian goods.

By the Warring States period (475–221 BC), decorative lacquer found greater acceptance in the embellishment of ceremonial offerings to the gods, the decoration of coffins and on musical instruments used in ancient rituals. Although the period is characterized as one of superb craftsmanship, the artisans lacked the ability to develop forms and decoration unique to the lacquer medium and instead turned to the solid shapes and patterns of earlier cast bronze vessels. During the short life of the Qin Dynasty (221–207 BC), an important philosophical transition began to occur: objects once made explicitly for ceremonial use began to be viewed for their material beauty and emotional appeal. The personal possession of lacquered goods soon came to be regarded as the objectification of emotion which, in turn, inspired the admiration and awe of others and laid the foundation for social status based on the ownership of material goods.

This significant change in societal values led to a blossoming of the arts and crafts during the Han Dynasty (206 BC–AD 220), as artists began to express their feelings of conquest and control over the material world. The introduction of rationalism, perhaps as an outgrowth of Confucian thought, slowly merged many of the primitive myths and magical beliefs with verifiable legends and historical personalities. In the process, gods were slowly humanized and extraordinary tales explained in an attempt to make the step from mortal to immortal an attainable reality. With the temptation of eternal rule placed before him, the Emperor Han Wudi sent emissaries on a search for an 'elixir of life'. In a sense lacquer answered this call, albeit on a symbolic level, for it was now widely praised for its power to protect and preserve. This mystical belief was bolstered by the use of *zhusha* (cinnabar), which was considered to be fundamental to Daoist alchemy. Regularly administered to unwitting believers as a longevity potion, it contained mercury, which in fact often had the unfortunate effect of sending its most vehement proponents to a premature afterlife.

Nevertheless, the new interest in the marvels of nature and the vitality of the human spirit that accompanied the Han period had a dramatic effect on ornamentation in all of the visual and decorative arts. The geometric ornamentation common to earlier works in lacquer gradually softened to include flowing cloud patterns suggestive of heaven and immortality, among which both imaginary and earthly animals were freely mixed.

The early Tang period, in the seventh century AD, is noteworthy for the opening of the insular Chinese culture to outside influences, permitting an enormous influx of foreign ideas, clothing, music, art and religion. The arrival of exotic silver vessels from the Near East brought tremendous demand among the privileged classes for similar items. As a consequence, the lacquer crafts, which looked to metal-smithing for inspiration, were also greatly influenced. The free adaptation of many visual motifs found on silver vessels made lacquer extremely popular, as well as an important intermediary influence in the application of silver designs to ceramics.

The introduction of the *qiangjin* inlay technique is a prime example of an attempt to transfer the patterns characteristic of metalsmithing to the lacquer arts. *Qiangjin* was a direct outgrowth of the chasing methods used on silver vessels and required the engraving or channelling of fine linear designs into the lacquer surface. These were then filled with flat sheets of gold or gold wire and brilliantly polished. Attempts to simulate punching techniques can also be seen in lacquer of the period, represented by rows of fine inlaid dots. This extravagant use of silver and gold suddenly raised the ornamental possibilities of lacquer goods to a new level and brought an equally dramatic increase in the value of the object. The considerable cost of precious metal inlays proved prohibitive for many and, as a result, lacquer also began to be painted with silver and gold designs to resemble the *qiangjin* technique.

In an attempt to refine the craft further and to diversify its use, new methods were continually being explored. The bodiless dry-lacquer technique, known in Chinese as *tuotai xiang*, was found to be especially well suited to the making of large decorative objects and sculptures without the need for the excessive weight of a large inner support. In this method, layers of silk were spread over a wooden or clay mould and repeatedly coated with the refined resin. In rural areas, burlap or other coarse fabrics were often substituted for silk when it proved too costly or was unavailable. Once the layers had hardened, the inner core was removed, resulting in an exceptionally lightweight object. This technique was frequently used to construct hollow-core Buddhist statues. As a result, mythological animals, deities and even Buddha figures could be made in large quantities using the same internal form. More detailed features were then added to the hardened figure, using a thick malleable paste composed of wood powder mixed with the natural polymer.

From the Southern Song period onward, beginning in the twelfth century, the delicate technique of carved lacquer found its way into the artisanal repertoire. First used during the eighth and ninth centuries in the fabrication of armour, saddles, shields and other armaments, carving brought a new sculptural dimension to decorative lacquerwares. This style was especially favoured in Beijing during the Yongle period (AD 1403–24) of the Ming Dynasty, during which time artists once again turned to the archaic forms of China's vast bronze casting traditions for their inspiration. After the painstaking application of hundreds of individual coats, which were needed to build a thick resinous base, lyrical designs were carved into the surface, revealing its exceptional depth. The method achieved even greater acclaim with the introduction of a polychrome process that further highlighted the exceptional carving. By making the incisions at a slight angle and cutting through alternating colour layers of black, red or yellow, artisans achieved greater richness and dimension of the sculptural form. The first carved lacquer motifs were variations of *tixi* patterns, which resemble scrolling heart shapes. These proved particularly popular on carved trays, bowls, cups and covered boxes.

Carved pictorial lacquerware was perfected during the early Ming Dynasty, drawing its initial references from natural fauna and flora. In time flowers, birds, dragons, representations of children and heavenly pavilions were all integrated into complex landscapes. The smallest objects, with the most detailed scenes, generally drew the highest praise, reflecting the Chinese love of miniature self-contained worlds. This tradition was further exemplified in the arts of bamboo, ivory and bone carving, which transformed intricately detailed narrative scenes into objects for serene contemplation.

In general, the ongoing development of the lacquer arts brought increasingly complex designs rendered in deeper relief by more experienced and self-assured hands. The techniques known as *tianqi*, *moxian* and *baibaokan* are all variations of decorative surface treatments that achieved much acclaim in their time. *Tianqi* is a variation of the *qiangjin* method that dates from the Southern Song period, characterized by the engraving of parallel lines in the lacquer surface. The dual incisions are filled with precious metal and the space between the two finished with a contrasting lacquer. Secondly, *moxian,* meaning 'polish reveal', is created with raised outlines representing the overall design. The low areas are then filled with coloured lacquers until they rise above the outline. When all of the colours have been completed, the surface is polished to a smooth consistency. The third decorative technique, much associated with Chinese lacquer furniture and folding screens, and widely used in today's export market, is *baibaokan* or 'hundred precious things' inlay. It is immediately recognizable for its high sculptural relief, which is used to render images of elegantly robed women and playful children scattered among ornately carved pavilions and gardens. The quality of this work has steadily declined since its initial popularity during the Qing Dynasty (1644–1911), to the point where it is now regularly scorned and ridiculed as a tourist craft of questionable taste.

The labour-intensive nature of fine lacquerwork and the materials required for its production have always made it an impractical medium for the single artisan. As a consequence, lacquer production was structured around group workshops and the division of labour skills from a very early period. In this manner, an individual artisan performing a specialized task was responsible for one stage in the production of a large number of individual pieces. This system was already well established by the Han Dynasty, as documented in the book

The inlay artists pictured here from the Chengdu Lacquer Ware Arts and Crafts Factory work intuitively, without pre-existing patterns or the mechanical transfer of designs. These finely crafted boxes, which take many months to complete, are examples of the very few large and complex works that will be produced during the year.

Discourses on Salt and Iron dating from 80 BC, in which it is noted that a single lacquered cup or bowl might require the skills of a hundred artisans and be worth ten times that of a similar vessel in bronze. Despite a laborious process and high price, well-organized workshops were able to produce an impressive quantity of well-made lacquer goods to satisfy the steadily growing demand.

Official workshops, or *Yuyong jian*, were established from an early period to oversee the production of a wide range of textiles, furniture and crafts for Imperial use, as well as for members of its court. The establishment of the first Imperial workshop in Beijing occurred shortly after the transfer of the capital from Changan in 1421. One of

the most prestigious was known as *Guiyuan chang,* or the 'Orchard Workshop', which was responsible for producing many fine pieces of carved lacquer furniture. Surviving documents make it clear that numerous lacquer-producing centres co-existed throughout the country. These were part of a unified handicraft market that ensured widespread availability of famous regional goods. Lacquerwares from Suzhou and Guangzhou (formerly Canton) both received high marks among dealers in the decorative arts, who referred disparagingly to the quality of the average lacquer goods produced in Beijing. Today it is difficult to ascertain with certainty the exact origins of many lacquered wares and one must look at technical features for significant clues.

Chengdu in Sichuan Province has enjoyed a long history of lacquer manufacturing beginning in the Warring States period. During the Western Han era its workshop produced thousands of pieces for the Imperial Palace, as well as the local elite, gaining the reputation as China's preeminent lacquer capital. The tomb of the Marquis of Dai excavated in 1973 in Changsha, Hunan Province, has yielded many fine examples of lacquered ewers and wine cups produced in Chengdu. Its acclaimed workshop came under government control during the middle years of the Western Han Dynasty and was instrumental in supplying foreign markets. Recent excavations have uncovered Chengdu lacquerwares at sites as far away as Korea.

Today artisans of the Chengdu Lacquer Ware Arts and Crafts Factory faithfully reproduce a variety of plates, bowls and covered boxes inspired by their ancient predecessors. Hidden away in a maze of small *hutong* or alleyways, the lacquer workshops comprise several modest buildings overlooking tranquil residential courtyards. All their work involves indigenous painted and inlay lacquer styles rooted in the history of the region. Unlike many other arts and crafts factories that copy styles with no particular emphasis on quality or authenticity, the artisans at the Chengdu Lacquer Ware workshop have begun to focus on their own artistic heritage. The motifs they use are excellent examples of the earliest styles of geometric decoration and low relief carving discovered in the area. Tremendous inspiration has come from hunting and reaping scenes found on the stamped brick walls of many Sichuan tombs dating from the late Han period. These loosely composed narrative scenes appear to combine depictions of both real and mythological subjects. Their influence is easily seen on today's painted lacquer platters and bowls, which incorporate similar animals and birds.

Many of the more sophisticated Sichuan lacquerwares are modelled after works from the Tang Dynasty, continuing the complex and expensive techniques of *qiangjin* and *moxian.* These include variations of black stacking boxes, ranging in size from eleven to over fifty centimetres in diameter. The smaller models are inlaid with abstract silver foliage patterns complemented by additional touches of red lacquer. The largest, which take many months to perfect, are inlaid with highly elaborate silver phoenix and dragon motifs. The underlying core for most Sichuan lacquers, including cups, bowls and platters, is made of wood which has been turned on a lathe to achieve a perfect shape. This is the case with many of the decorative boxes as well, although the carving of complex or irregular forms is still done by hand. Each piece then undergoes a rigorous and time-consuming procedure alternating wet-sanding with lacquering until a flawlessly smooth surface has been created. For the simplest painted Chengdu wares this can amount to between twelve and twenty individual coats. For carved objects, as many as one hundred separate layers must be applied. Sichuan's hot and humid climate is an ideal environment for the preparation of lacquer crafts, which require constant humidity to harden. During the intense heat of the summer months, much of the work in Chengdu can be carried on outside, where rows of washing troughs have been built for the wet-sanding procedures.

By contrast, the lacquerware now produced in Beijing is based on the ornate Imperial styles of the Ming and Qing Dynasties, renowed for their elaborate and detailed carvings. This was the technique particularly favoured by the Emperor Qianlong, whose patronage filled the Imperial Palace with carved lacquer vases, screens, chairs and other grandiose furnishings. The Beijing Carved Lacquer Ware Factory produces many one-of-a-kind and specially commissioned objects destined for first-class hotels throughout Asia. Their artisans are trained in an apprentice system similar to that practised centuries ago; they are taught to recognize the noteworthy characteristics of the famous carvers who produced such goods before them.

Much of the recent growth in popularity of Chinese lacquerware can be attributed to increased tourism, which has led to a slow revival of many traditional arts and crafts during the past decade. The gradual recognition that such items are highly appreciated by foreign visitors has brought a significant increase in their availability and overall quality. From intricately carved snuff bottles to boxes, plates, trays and teapots, lacquerware remains an enduring symbol of China's ancient arts and crafts traditions.

CLAY

When the four corners of the earth collapsed,
the land split open and the heavens stood no longer,
Nuwa melted coloured rock to patch the sky above
and cast men in clay to inhabit the yellow earth below

– Ancient reference to Nüwa, the female creator of earth

The Chinese people have long maintained a close affinity with their soil. In literature and song, folk tale and verse, the yellow earth of Shaanxi Province has for centuries inspired men of letters as well as men of the land to dream of their distant origins. Throughout history this vast territory, cradled by both the Wei and the Yellow Rivers, has been referred to as the mother of the Chinese people and it is on and of this land that China's earliest culture was formed. The best preserved of the early Neolithic settlements is that of Banpo (c. 4000–3000 BC), near present-day Xian, where artisan-potters excelled in coil, slab and hand-modelled vessels of low-fired earthenware. The emerging layout of this excavated riverside village indicates a high level of community planning, with areas carefully defined for residential dwellings, a community house, a burial site, as well as numerous pottery workshops fitted with simple up-draught kilns.

The widespread development of the Neolithic culture throughout the Yellow River Valley, extending to Shandong Province in the east and along the Wei

(left) *A stone rubbing representing Huang Di, Lord of the Yellow Earth.* (right) *Rendering of a Banpo dwelling, indicating a conscious division of internal space for specific activities. Constructed of upright posts, walls of wattle and a thatched roof. Banpo, Shaanxi Province.*

Early 'swimming fish' and decorations resembling the human face were made with painted slips on earthenware vessels at the Banpo site as early as 5000 BC.

River to Gansu Province in the west, assured great diversity in the form and decoration of early ceramic wares. The simplest pots from the Yellow River Basin were crafted for basic utilitarian needs in greyware and impressed with cord motifs. Other finer, smoothly burnished examples have been found in Shaanxi Province, decorated with coloured slips in white, rust and black. The ceramists of Banpo were adept at a technique referred to as 'painted pottery', a term that originated with finds at the nearby Yangshao site. These vessels were embellished with

geometric fish motifs and stylized human heads, which can be traced to early religious beliefs. The fish is one of the oldest symbols in use on Chinese arts and crafts and is often depicted on primitive designs representing the cyclical nature of the universe.

The varying composition of Chinese soil, rich in sedimentary clays, kaolin and fire clay, has contributed to an outstanding variety of high-fired artisanal ceramics. For thousands of years, clay's tactile malleability has made it an appealing and evocative material for artisan and layman alike and

has spawned specialized domestic industries that to this day are renowned around the world. The widespread use of the word 'China', generally designating Chinese porcelain, is indicative of the tremendous acclaim such works attracted in the West. Western manufacturers sought to copy Chinese designs, not so much for the beauty of the patterns but for the quality of the porcelain that they came to represent. Not only was the porcelain stone used to make the vessels extremely abundant in China, but also the high-temperature kilns necessary to fire the wares had not been matched in the West. Thus, fine Chinese porcelains developed a reputation for excellence throughout the world and now grace the collections of many celebrated museums.

Such recognized and valued vessels form only a small portion of China's long and important ceramic heritage. Rarely collected or documented are the many playful and utilitarian ceramic objects and containers still produced for daily life. These are the works born of necessity and

The long or 'Dragon' kiln was the primary style used throughout southern China. Dating from the Warring States period, the Dragon kiln was wood-fired, achieving temperatures in excess of 1200 degrees centigrade.

The mantou kiln, named after its resemblance to the steamed bread of northern China, was coal-fired and achieved temperatures of 1370 degrees centigrade.

A vendor of painted clay toys and masks in Fengxiang, Shaanxi Province.

maintained over many centuries by generations of Chinese labourers, who view their creations not as art but merely as the fulfilment of a social or domestic need. As a result, their creations are rarely signed and their use tends to be limited to the unique habits, customs and ceremonies of a given region. For this reason Chinese clay crafts are as varied as the geographic locales from which they originate.

The preoccupation with engendering the good wishes of the gods has led to their representation in many forms. Homes in southwestern China still display roughly fashioned sculptures of protective gods and deities in blackened low-fired clay. Some are hand-moulded by the residents themselves and then baked on the oven or stove. Others are made in local roof tile or brick factories by labourers, who quickly fashion left-over bits of clay into a simple door or hearth god at the end of the day. It is not uncommon for older men, long retired from the potteries, to pass their idle hours making handcrafted animals or figures based on models from the horoscope, or characters from local opera lore. Such objects are then given away or sold for tiny sums to safeguard the home or used as entertainment for the children.

Folk artisans selling earthen and clay toys from temporary stands first appeared during the Song Dynasty (AD 960–1279). Many of these toys were offered as prizes in simple gambling and festival games in the local markets and some featured movable parts or incorporated sounds such as rattles or whistles, traditions which continue to this day. The most popular toys, however, were small dolls known as *Mohele,* which were sold in large quantities during the festivities of the seventh day of the seventh month that celebrate the mythological meeting of the weaving maiden and the herdboy. Unlike many other clay toys, *Mohele* were actually dressed in tiny handmade clothes. Their primary purpose was to aid the local women in soliciting wisdom from the weaving maiden and thus increase their chances of bearing a male child.

Fengxiang painted clay animals often feature moving ears or tails mounted on tiny springs to sway and bob when touched. (from top) *Tiger, black ox and tiger mask.*

Today, many varieties of clay toys can only be found during the weeks and months just prior to the annual Spring Festival when a creative frenzy begins to grip each village. Tremendous time and effort is given over to festival preparations, using techniques that have remained essentially unchanged for centuries. Most clay toys begin with local earth, which has been mixed with hemp, cotton rags or boiled paper pulp. The substance is then hand formed or pressed into a double-sided wood mould to achieve the desired shape. This hollow moulding process leaves a cavity into which small stones or beans are often placed to produce a rattle when the two halves are finally joined together. The new toy is then left outside to bake in the midday sun or placed on the hearth or near the oven to dry, after which more detailed features are carved into the clay surface to define further the intrinsic character or form. When the basic body of the toy is resolved, a primer of homemade gesso or resin is applied. The actual composition of this sealant varies widely according to province, but normally involves the boiling of soot or brick dust to create a thick glaze. Such undercoatings provide a more uniform surface upon which brighter colours, mixed with glue or egg white, are added to create a light lustre finish. The clay dolls of Xiaogou and Lingmongzhu villages in Shangdong Province typify this process.

The elaborately painted clay toys, masks and reliefs of Fengxiang, Qian and Ansai in Fengxiang County, west of Xian, have been continuously and lovingly crafted for over 600 years and offer a fine example of the artistic licence enjoyed by many rural artisans. The Fengxiang toad, a popular clay subject there, has been modified and manipulated over the years, so that it now bears more resemblance to a smiling rodent or squirrel. The exact identities of

other Fengxiang animals are equally hard to determine, as imaginative craftsmen freely grant their creations exaggerated features in response to an ongoing evolution of local folklore.

A variety of other popular mythological figures are also produced in Shaanxi Province, representing the Eight Immortals and characters derived from the Chinese classic *Xi You Ji (Journey to the West)*. The imaginary *qiling,* comprising the head of a unicorn, body of a deer, the tail of an ox and horses' hooves, is regularly depicted in its customary role delivering a son. The legendary herd boy, traditionally modelled riding his favourite cow, is also a common theme. Each of these animals is carefully painted with well-known symbolic motifs, including lucky flowers such as peonies, longevity peaches, lotus flowers and pomegranates.

Shaanxi and Hunan Provinces are well known for making festival whistles. On the fifteenth day of the first and seventh lunar months, villages in Hunan's Fuqiu County hold the 'Grandma Temple Fair'. For two weeks, peasants from neighbouring areas come to enjoy the festive atmosphere and elderly women pray for grandchildren. Thumb-sized bird whistles are sold as presents for the grandchildren left at home, while others are tossed by women into the river to cast a wish. A local rhyme assures the grandmothers of satisfaction:

Give me a clay coo-coo, Grandma;
Back home you'll have a grandchild.

Like many other clay toys, the birds originate in one small village. Nearly every one of the seven hundred households in Fuqiu County engages in the making of some type of toy. To simplify the production process many toys are made in large quantities at one sitting. This is the case with the clay bird whistles. The front portions of the decorative whistles are press-moulded by the dozen while the backs, featuring the vent hole, are made by hand. Once assembled, they are left to dry on the hearth for several days. They are then low-fired in a combination of rice husks and sawdust, which blackens the clay and requires that the finished toys be painted and sealed.

Easily recognized throughout China are the *Dafu*, or 'big fatties', which are made in Wuxi in Jiangsu Province. They are commonly sold in pairs, representing a boy and girl. Traditionally *Dafu* are made by press-moulding local clay and then low-firing the raw forms. They are then painted with colourful enamels depicting clothing, lucky symbols and auspicious objects. The origin of the clay fatties comes from local legend, which tells of a fierce beast emerging from the forests at the base of Mount Huishan. Stronger and more frightening than either a tiger or a wolf, the beast terrorized the land and devoured the local residents. But one day a child, with fantastic powers to subdue demons and monsters, quickly killed the raging beast to save the remaining citizens. Using the rich clay dug from the mountainside the peasants created a sculpture in the boy's honour and named it *Ahfu* or 'the lucky one'. Over time, the image of *Ahfu*, or *Dafu* as he has since come to be known, has served to protect hunters and farmers from danger through its mysterious properties.

Wuxi artists continue to rely on the clay from Mount Huishan in the creation of *Ahfu*, as well as a variety of other colourful figures and animals, because of its resistance to cracking during the drying process. The mythical black ox is one of the most popular Wuxi animals, since it is directly related to the prosperity of the villages. It is said that whoever touches the hooves of the ox will be sure to have land, while touching the head will protect a family from worry.

Painted clay girl, or Duan Nue, decorated with a stylized dove and bearing the characters for fortune, luck, longevity and happiness, flanked by a pair of Afu, or lucky figures, inscribed with the characters of longevity and luck. Wuxi, Zhejiang Province. h.11 cm and 6 cm

Other auspicious practices to ensure good health, fortune and longevity continue to be played out in China's domestic architecture. Throughout the country artisans engage in the making of decorative clay tiles that not only provide a practical function by capping the eaves but also serve to placate the spirits. Early guidelines for proper building methods were outlined in the Song Dynasty book, *Yingzao Fashi* ('Building Standards'), which proved influential for many centuries. As a result, roof tiles embellished with the images of the four gods of direction were installed to show respect and to reaffirm the proper alignment of the house. Thus, east was represented by a green dragon, west by a white tiger, south by *Zhuque* (a mythical bird), and north by *Xuanwu* (a mythical tortoise). Additional tile motifs included the symbol *shuangxi* for 'double happiness' and a variety of birds, butterflies and flower designs.

The Chinese are tenacious believers in the power of the supernatural to grant happiness and good fortune, and *fengshui* (geomancy) also remains vitally important in Chinese architectural tradition to protect the family from harm. To ensure the proper orientation of the building site, a knowledgeable geomancer is always summoned during the initial planning. Symbolic offerings are then made and incantations are recited to placate the spirits during the most important stages of construction. Such perfunctory displays of modesty and devotion have long been a Chinese characteristic and grow out of the belief that unbridled ambition or greed could engender the spite of ghosts, who might then subject them to a lifetime of misery and suffering.

Thus it comes as no surprise that a mysterious monk, who appeared one day in the village of Yixing crying 'Riches and honours for sale!', was greeted with laughter and cool indifference by the local inhabitants. In time, however, their curiosity prevailed and the village elders were led to a place in the nearby hills where they were shown rich deposits of clay in such vivid colours as to resemble fine brocade.

This tale comprises the first documented reference to the village of Yixing, as noted in the *Yangxien Minghu Xi* dating from the Wanli period (AD 1573–1619). Just as Jingdezhen in Jiangxi Province was known for its production of extraordinary porcelain, Yixing was, and remains, the centre for artisanal ceramics in China. It is thought that during the Warring States period Fan Li, the Minister of the Kingdom of Yue, settled there with the famous beauty, Xi Shi, and, as a pastime, began to make ceramics. Since then he has been worshipped as the patron saint of potters and is believed to watch over the village of Yixing.

It is not known with certainty when the Yixing potteries first achieved broad recognition. However, prior to the sixteenth century, they were best known for the production of coarse utilitarian ceramics such as planters, pickling vessels and urns. Sometime in the middle of the Ming Dynasty (AD 1368–1644), a monk from the nearby Jinsha Temple began to associate with the Yixing potters and learned from them the mixing and seasoning of the local clay. He then introduced a method for forming teapots out of a single lump and stamped them with his fingerprint as an identifying mark. This method was continued and further developed when the servant of a visiting scholar learned the hand-modelling technique and remained in Yixing to become an admired potter, renowned for his irregularly shaped chestnut-coloured pots. Word of the naturally coloured clay pots quickly spread and others soon joined him.

Unlike most Chinese arts and crafts, new or old, Yixing teapots have always been signed or stamped by their maker. For this reason, much is known about the individual potters of Yixing with regard to their artistic development. Because many of the early ceramists had no calligraphic training, the task of signing was regularly assigned to a member of the group whose penmanship was of sufficient quality.

By the Wanli period, the simple, unpretentious teapots being produced in Yixing began to be viewed as the embodiment of virtue and beauty by a growing Chinese literati, who eagerly sought to collect the humble vessels as works of art. Although four early master potters can be identified, no known examples of their work exist today. Nevertheless, early copies give us a sense of the rustic and contemplative beauty they possessed.

The ceramic arts of Yixing never received Imperial patronage in the manner of other ceramic and porcelain centres. It is presumed that the many irregularities and the unglazed nature of the earthen coloured clays, the very qualities that attracted the Chinese literati, were viewed as inappropriate for the Imperial Court. Support came instead from poets, scholars and artists, who saw in the pieces parallels to their own reflections on the nature of beauty. The gifted Hangzhou scholar, Chen Mansheng (AD 1768–1822), designed eighteen teapot styles while serving as a magistrate in Yixing and hired the leading ceramists to manufacture them for him. He and his friends inscribed thousands of pots with poetic musings. His poetic inscriptions on Yixing wares led to the use of the term *Mansheng hu* to define a calligraphic teapot in his style. This close collaboration enjoyed by the scholars and craftsmen set an important precedent for Chinese crafts by effectively elevating the artisanal pottery of Yixing to that of an esoteric art.

With the maturing of the Yixing style during the late Ming Dynasty, the highly collectible purple-brown teapots (*zisha hu*) began to find large export markets in Thailand and Japan, where they were particularly influential and were copied by the Banko and Tokoname potters. During the seventeenth and eighteenth centuries, Yixing teapots also found their way to Europe and were highly instrumental in the development of unglazed English and Dutch stoneware.

The conception and interpretation of a Yixing teapot's subject matter ranks as important as the meticulous crafting itself. Naturalistic forms gain the greatest attention today, but simple geometric pots – many with poetic inscriptions – are also highly desirable. Over hundreds of years, the artisan potters of Yixing have repeatedly turned to a handful of traditional themes on which to base their works. These include variations of young and old bamboo, represented either as tender sprouts or hardened stalks, symbolic seeds and fruits, and numerous birds and animals. Geometric teapots often take the form of ancient bronze vessels, bricks and decorative tiles. In addition, the handles of each pot have important historical

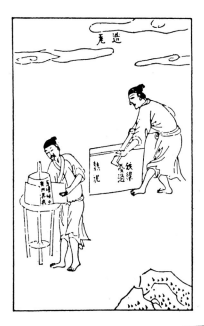

Seventeenth-century woodblock prints depicting the manufacture of clay roof tiles. Using a bell-shaped mould, slabs of clay are wrapped around the exterior. The mould is then collapsed and removed, leaving a dried clay form that can be broken into four concave tiles.

'Lu Ban's Secret Chart', a reference for carpenters describing auspicious charms that can be hidden in a home to engender good fortune. A cassia leaf hidden in the column brackets will bring scholarly success; a boat with the bow pointed inward brings riches; and a pine bough ensures long life.

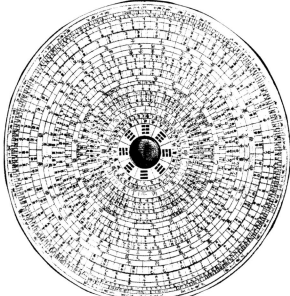

An ancient geomancer's compass, known as a luopan, in etched bamboo. This was the type commonly used for the orientation of building sites and the correct positioning of their related furnishings. It consisted of three rotating discs, symbolizing Heaven, Earth and Man, with the symbols of the Eight Triagrams at the centre.

precedents and are usually well integrated into the design itself.

To each of these considerations is joined the concern for the actual clay, which is composed of coarse particles of kaolin, quartz and mica, with high concentrations of iron and silicon. The technical characteristics of Yixing clays place them between porcelain and pottery wares, and in many respects make them superior to porcelain. Yixing teapots suffer minimal contraction during firing, and their highly innovative forms are therefore not distorted. The degree of water absorption and porosity of the fired wares is also relatively low, explaining the ability of the pot to protect the colour, fragrance and taste of the tea within. In addition, the form of the clay particles has been found to be scale-like rather than granular, making the pots extremely adaptable to sudden temperature changes and unlikely to crack. Similarly, a Yixing pot that is filled with boiling water does not quickly conduct the heat outward, thus avoiding any chance of scalded hands.

There are generally three recognized colour classifications to Yixing wares, within which one can still find a great diversity of natural tones. The first is known as *zishani* ('purple clay') and in its raw state ranges from light purple to purplish-red, deepening to purplish-brown and purplish-black after firing. The second, referred to as *lüni* ('green clay'), has a greyish-white or greyish-green cast, turning to light grey or greyish-yellow. The third classification is *hongni* ('red clay'), which begins as reddish-brown, turning to greyish-black after firing. While all of these colours originate locally, it is the purple clay of Dingshu County which has historically overshadowed each of the others in popularity. It is often modified by the addition of other minerals to produce softened reds, yellows, greens and golds. Many contemporary ceramists take advantage of this potential by creating vessels bearing multi-coloured decorations, which need no additional glazing.

The continued popularity of Yixing teapots today certainly stems from the exceptional variety of evocative forms in which they are crafted, as well as their remarkable ability to accentuate and protect the flavour of the delicate tea within. With proper care even tea left overnight in hot summer temperatures will not sour. To achieve this, Yixing teapots are never washed. Instead, the old leaves are simply removed and the pots are carefully rinsed in cold water. In this manner, each develops a rich inner patina and an individual character unmatched by a new pot. Countless stories have been told of the lament of artists and poets alike who have been moved to tears by the loss of such a vessel, as each Yixing teapot becomes a living record of all those, mighty and small, who have sipped its subtle flavours during a lifetime of service.

BAMBOO & WOOD

> *On the basis of period, new is better than old. On the basis of place, northern is not as good as southern. The wooden pieces of Yangzhou and the bamboo pieces of Suzhou can be said to be the best of all time, and hold first place throughout the empire*
>
> – Li Yu, *Random Notes on Times of Leisure*, 1671

One cannot pass a day in China without encountering an assortment of bamboo images or handmade bamboo goods – whether in the form of a classical ink painting, or the ubiquitous multi-story construction scaffolding of giant bamboo that encircles one of China's vast number of building sites; or perhaps an infant's chair replete with gracious arms and woven seat, or an exquisitely carved necklace. Bamboo is omnipresent in Chinese society. It is a material that evokes a multiplicity of emotion and meaning in the Chinese culture and has remained the most popular and respected subject for artists for hundreds of years. In poetry, bamboo has become a moving metaphor for endurance and virtue: its qualities always admirable, its form, when likened to a man, a symbol of aspiration. Consequently, images of bamboo can be found embroidered onto children's clothing and engraved in stone. Throughout history the difference between fame and failure for a visual artist has rested on his singular ability to capture the essence of bamboo in a few brilliant strokes of the brush. For this reason it has been said that a Chinese artist must first *become* bamboo before he can actually begin to paint it.

Bamboo is as ideal an artistic medium as it is utilitarian. It is highly impervious to both fire and water and its natural characteristic of cleaving easily in long

Bamboo ink painting from The Mustard Seed Garden, *a woodblock printed manual of painting techniques that first appeared in 1679.*

lengths makes it an exemplary weaving material. Once it is cut into splints, a variety of woven goods can be made to satisfy practically any daily need. The extreme flexibility of the outer layer of the young bamboo shoot is well suited to fine or delicate weaving techniques, while objects requiring hardness and durability are crafted with older stems after they have developed a tougher woody layer. As a result, basketry arts developed early in China, with specialized forms and finishes quickly evolving for every purpose. Vessels or containers destined to carry large goods are usually constructed with open-weave techniques that support great weights with a minimal use of material. These include baskets for fruits and vegetables, which benefit from the free circulation of air, and larger bamboo cages for the transport of chickens or ducks to the village market. Household baskets are regularly sold by vendors who parade through the city streets calling out their specialized wares, which often include a selection of small bamboo toys and pinwheels for children. Most pedlars come from rural basket-making communities where entire families have

Principal variations of bamboo weaves commonly found in Chinese basketry.

engaged in the refinement and perfection of a distinctive style over many generations.

The intricately wrapped porcelains of Chengdu in Sichuan Province continue a delicate and painstaking fabrication technique developed more than a century ago. Using porcelain shipped from the famous ceramics centre of Jingdezhen in Jiangsu Province, dyed bamboo filaments as fine as hair are woven around the porcelain objects to form durable and decorative coverings. Made entirely by hand in the local workshops, the bamboo-wrapped wares encompass a variety of handsomely coloured vases, jars and tea sets that are as functional as they are attractive. This particularly Sichuanese tradition of wrapping utilitarian vessels in bamboo was not originally limited to porcelain. Numerous examples of antique pewter wares exist, as well as wine pots which were also sheathed in the finely woven material.

Inspired by many surviving examples, as well as others unearthed in archaeological excavations, Sichuan artisans continue to produce bamboo handicrafts based on traditional models. Miniature stacking baskets resembling those once made to carry ceremonial foods are embellished with bright geometric butterflies and given new domestic uses. Sets of round nested boxes and multi-coloured bamboo hand-bags are modern adaptations of vernacular crafts that are being kept alive with the help of increased tourism and the growing popularity in the West for exotic handmade products.

Today small cottage industries continue to produce a wide variety of carved bamboo arts. While some remain purely decorative, others serve a daily function, such as chopsticks carved to resemble the 'Eight Immortals' and engraved with prosaic sayings and good wishes. Bamboo fans are also popular crafts found in Sichuan Province. The tough outer layers of mature bamboo are cut into wide staves, pierced and joined by a metal rivet or ring, and then vibrantly painted to resemble exotic plumed birds and brightly winged butterflies. Seen resting on a chair or table, such creations easily double as unique pieces of folk sculpture. Ranging in size from tiny pocket models to over 30 centimetres in length, these enchanting folding fans cool and refresh the user in this steamy province, much to the visual delight of onlookers. Other Sichuan fans bear hand-painted images of the long bearded masks of local *Chuan* opera characters, rendered on heavy black paper and glued to darkly stained bamboo ribs.

The folding fan, which remains most popular today, is widely believed to have originated in Korea, where it was first used by servants who could immediately tuck it away when called upon to render a service. Its introduction to China did not come until the tenth century AD, when it arrived by way of Japan, eventually becoming a mark of official rank and social position. During the Ming and Qing Dynasties the hand fan underwent tremendous refinement in both material and form, with folding paper and silk fans often lavishly painted by esteemed artists, or inscribed by the hand of an accomplished calligrapher.

Along the eastern coastal region many fans are made entirely of wood. China's rich diversity of fragrant and exotic woods has ensured both a prominent material and spiritual role in the artisanal traditions of the country. Predominant in Chinese crafts are sandalwood, boxwood, ebony, persimmon, redwood, red oak and birch. Because of the highly physical nature of woodworking, throughout history it was set apart from the higher arts as practised by the scholar officials. However, many woodcrafts, including furniture-making, were well enough respected within official circles for prized examples to be regularly presented as gifts to the Imperial Court.

Suzhou in Jiangsu Province has a long-standing reputation in the crafting of classical fans, with hundreds of independent craftsmen and workshops each turning out their own family variations. Perhaps most popular are the *tanxiang* or carved and pierced sandalwood fans carried by women during the summer months. Left completely unvarnished, they impart a gentle aroma when waved, thus sparing the local women the unpleasantries brought with excessive heat. As the summer comes to an end, the fragrant fans are returned to a drawer containing the woman's most cherished clothing, in the knowledge that the natural repellent properties of the sandalwood will protect it from bugs and moths until the following year.

Not far from Suzhou is the canal town of Wuxi, the legendary home of the decorative wooden comb. Once an integral part of a woman's daily toilette and dressing routine, specialized combs performed a variety of distinct functions. Versions intended for grooming were normally used in conjunction with a small porcelain jar, which held an oily fluid made from the fragrant wood shavings of a resinous tree that had been soaked in water. To prepare the hair, a woman first dipped her comb into this sticky substance, then drew it through the hair to add sheen and to fix it in its proper place. The pointed end, a characteristic feature of the long-handled Chinese comb, functioned as a pick to assist in the division of the hair for further parting or braiding. The straight dark hair common to Chinese women gave them an ideal opportunity to engage in complex styling techniques with the aid of assorted clips and combs. Such elaborate attempts at hairdressing once inspired highly descriptive names such as the 'Magpie Tail' and 'Falling from Horse' styles.

Today, many Wuxi combs have value beyond their original function and are collected for their elaborate designs, carefully hand-painted in enamel. Lucky and auspicious themes predominate, such as Shou Xing, the God of Longevity, who is portrayed in a variety of shapes and sizes. Brightly painted butterflies offer the wearer the possibility of two comb ridges ingeniously carved to follow the shape of the wings. Fish signifying abundance are also popular themes, either rendered individually or in the arms of a young boy who is recognized as the bearer of prosperity. Many decorative combs are supplied with silk cords to enable them to be worn around the neck as pendants or charms. From time to time, the artisans of Wuxi introduce new groups of combs, including characters from such ancient folktales as the *Maidens of the Moon Palace*. Each is packaged in a elegant brocade box replicating those once used to deliver combs to the Imperial Court during the early Qing Dynasty.

The creation of fragrant and exotic wood crafts is also a characteristic of many minority cultures. For the Dong, the fir tree is the focus of numerous ancient rituals, as

A young Chinese woman with a folding paper fan poses for a studio photographer. Early twentieth century.

well as the basis for their economic livelihood today. Their production of the famed tung oil, as well as numerous varnishes and lacquers, is highly regarded among Chinese artisans. The fir also constitutes the primary building material of the Dong. According

to tradition a family must plant a fir sapling to commemorate the birth of each child. As the child reaches the age of eighteen and marries, the matured tree is felled and offered as a symbolic contribution toward the building of a house for the new bride

and groom. For this reason the Dong refer to the firs as 'eighteen year trees'. Their lavish village 'Drum Towers', also constructed in fir, become annual focal points for elaborate dances and celebrations. The tower of Gaozhen village in Guizhou Province is particularly admired. Standing thirteen stories and carved with ornate dragons, phoenixes, flowers and birds, it is one of the masterpieces of wooden folk architecture and an important monument in the Dong practice of ancestor worship.

As a result of early sacred and mystical beliefs associated with death and the after-life, wooden idols were once carved by Chinese artisans to serve as guardian figures and guides to the world beyond. An abundance of such funerary figures has been found dating from the sixth and fifth centuries BC in tombs in Henan and Hubei Provinces, indicating that such wooden figures were becoming substitutes for human sacrifice. Finds from the southern state of Chu during the same period show a strong interest in both demonic and divine funerary idols, which served to portray this ancient civilization's complex beliefs in the mysterious spirit world. The inspiration for these haunting, half-human, half-animal wood carvings most probably evolved from earlier bronze castings of sacred animals. The composite creatures, many bearing protruding tongues and long twisting antlers, are thought to have been brightly lacquered to increase their startling effect.

Today, carved wood representations of ancient gods and deities are still found throughout the provinces on architectural ornamentation, on totems and in the form of elaborate masks. The Lahu people of southern Yunnan have long practised polytheism; they continue to erect wooden

(far left) *Fourth-generation basket pedlar from Chongqing County, Sichuan Province, loaded with his family wares.*

(left) *An elderly man lights his bamboo pipe. Kunming, Yunnan Province.*

(below) *Stacks of woven bamboo brooms and pans for winnowing rice wait for buyers at a village market in Sichuan Province.*

plaques carved with geometric designs intended to appease the master god Exia, whom they believe controls the future and fortunes of all mortals. As in the customs of many southwestern minority peoples, this practice of exaltation is closely tied to a rich oral tradition of music, storytelling and dance.

In both Miao and Dong communities, wooden totem poles are mounted to placate roaming animal spirits and other demons as part of ancient animist beliefs. These rituals reflect the basic conviction that spirits are not exclusive to humans but also reside in natural objects such as rocks, trees and streams. Such ideas found a following among many of China's tribal people, who for centuries have struggled against hostile elements for their survival. Both illness and natural disasters were thought to be the work of malicious spirits, who could only be appeased by the village shaman. For this reason, one of the most important roles of the shaman was, and remains, his ability to resolve any lingering conflicts in the souls of the dead and to help in their passage to the afterlife. Terrible consequences were certain to result from a soul precariously caught between the two worlds. In the course of performing his special role as a spiritual medium, the shaman himself becomes possessed by external forces to ensure the departure or elimination of the ill-natured influences.

This frightening vision of life, death and the spirit world is actively played out through a form of indigenous opera known for its carved and painted wood masks. Created over 3,000 years ago, the performance known as the *Nuo xi* has undergone many centuries of evolution and change. First devised as a ritual to drive away

Illustration of a carved wood guardian figure excavated from a Warring States tomb (480–221 BC).

Sketches of two Di xi masks from Guizhou Province. Constructed in separate pieces to simulate the military armour of the Ming Dynasty, their ferocious faces were effective in frightening opposing armies.

their predecessors, farmers from the community don ceremonial clothing, along with the expressively carved masks and dance, to an improvised beat accompanied by gongs, drums and cymbals. The performance site may be a central room in an individual home, a spacious courtyard, or a village square. As with other forms of Chinese opera, the female roles in the *Nuo xi* are traditionally played by men.

The Yi and Bouyei minorities in Guizhou have developed their own variations of *Nuo xi*, thought by many to be closer to the original, more primitive ceremony. The masks, carved from the local azalea and lacquer trees, are characterized by wild stares and contorted, crying mouths. After the carving is complete, the masks are brushed with scalded cooking oil, dramatically darkening the wood, before final details are applied in powdered lime.

Regardless of the version, *Nuo* masks can be divided into three basic characterizations. Among the most popular are those of the spirits and gods, which take their visual inspiration from the existing deities depicted in local temples. Their super-human representation still has the power to enthral audiences, who look to the gods for abundant harvests and the protection of family and property. The second category of characters is composed of heroic figures drawn from ancient novels. These are the mortals who succeed against all odds and through acts of selflessness and bravery eventually triumph over evil. The third group consists of various merchants, peasants and tradesmen from daily life, who form the basic fabric of the story and often become the victims of villainous forces and simple deceits.

Another popular operatic form found in southwest China, loosely derived from the *Nuo xi*, is called *Di xi*. It was practised by the army during the early Ming Dynasty

pestilence and evil, *Nuo xi* became known as the 'Masked Dance' or the 'Dance of the Twelve Gods' during the Han Dynasty as local folk tales and peasant dances were integrated into the original performance. Such additions gave the ceremonies a popular reference, drawing larger crowds who could understand the actions through the context of their own folk traditions. These modifications, based on the unique lore of the individual villages, allowed widely differing interpretations of the opera to flourish.

Performances of the *Nuo xi*, although increasingly rare, may still be seen in remote villages of Guizhou Province, where they are believed to exorcize evil spirits that might interfere with a recent birth or marriage. In the same manner as under Emperor Zhu Yuanzhang. An effort was made to unify rebelling provinces in the south by dispatching the army in the costumes of their favourite opera characters. When the opposing forces saw the fiercely attired army approach, they were frightened into quick submission. For this reason the essence of *Di xi* is always historical, rather than spiritual or divine. Its themes have been drawn from historical battles, acts of heroism and the rise and fall of the dynasties. As with *Nuo xi, Di xi* has grown to include more diverse themes and personalities from popular folk tales, so that a complete set of masks capable of representing the entire repertoire might amount to over eight hundred individual characters.

Di masks are easily recognized by their severe stares, brightly painted angular features and tight grimaces. They are consistently adorned with decorative crowns embellished with intertwined dragons, serpents and animal faces. Many older versions incorporate long moustaches and beards of human hair, which add to their ferocity and dramatic appeal. As compared with *Nuo* masks, which fit over the face, *Di* masks are worn tied to the forehead, giving the performers a towering height. The long, pointed ears that adorn all *Di* masks are made separately and attached to the main section with jute in simulation of ancient battle armour. To these ears, many actors attach long pheasant feathers, which wave wildly during the performance. Miniature versions of *Di* masks are often made as children's toys and are sold by vendors during local festivals.

It has been suggested that the stylized, almost mechanical, movements that characterize China's many varieties of operatic theatre originated with early puppet plays. Puppetry, like provincial opera, has a long and prestigious history in

Two examples of intricately carved leather shadow puppets that are intended to express effectively the complexity of each character in their stylized lines.

China and has been a principal source of entertainment for Chinese children and adults for centuries. Legend credits its formal development to Yang Shi during the reign of King Mu in the Zhou Dynasty. His skills were said to be so complete and his puppets so life-like that they could execute amazing acrobatic feats. When he was summoned to the Imperial Palace to perform at a state dinner, the Emperor suddenly stopped the entertainment mid-way and ordered the execution of the master puppeteer. When questioned as to the cause of his displeasure, the Emperor responded that some of the actors had disrespectfully winked at the ladies of his court. Yang Shi, fearful for his life, quickly cut the puppets open to reveal their contents of rags and straw, thus convincing

the Emperor that it was only a trick of his imagination.

Today the art of puppetry continues in many variations, though it is perhaps the *pi ying* ('leather shadow') puppets that are best known around the world. Legend dates the conception of shadow theatre to the Western Han Dynasty and the grieving Emperor Han Wudi, who had just suffered the loss of his favourite concubine, the beautiful Li Furen. At the behest of one of his aides, who suggested he could bring her back to life, Han Wudi sat each night in his darkened room as the spirit of the concubine appeared behind a gauze screen acting out the events of her life. Thus was born the idea for Chinese shadow theatre. It is likely that the first puppets were cut from paper in a manner and style resembling the rural paper cuts found throughout Shaanxi Province. These were often glued to lanterns and windows, creating natural shadows that danced by the flickering light of a candle or oil lamp. In parts of southern China this particular art of puppetry is still referred to as 'paper shadows'. However, by the Song Dynasty the puppets had achieved a degree of popularity and most were being cut from paper-thin pieces of translucent ox or donkey skin and carefully dyed to highlight their physical form and fanciful attire.

During the Yuan Dynasty both costumes and facial features were modified to resemble the robes and masks found in live opera. The faces of the earthly characters were represented in profile, with their bodies turned in three-quarter frontal pose. Heavenly personages were generally rendered frontally and houses, temples and landscapes were cut to imply perspective. Such disparity in visual treatment, combined with the strong facial caricatures borrowed from traditional opera, helped to identify the roles of the puppets for rural viewers.

As many as eight people were required to stage a shadow puppet performance, including storytellers, musicians and the puppeteers themselves. Despite the large number of pieces involved in staging a shadow play, the lightweight materials made it an art highly suited to touring. This was particularly popular at the end of the Qing Dynasty when, during the tenth lunar month after the completion of the peasants' labours, many men took to the road as touring shadow-players. A simple screen would be assembled in a town square, with the performance beginning at dusk. Such non-professional troupes often created their own stories, marrying historical and military

Villagers don ceremonial clothing and Nuo xi *masks to perform an improvised story of demonic trickery and deceit, captivating the local audience. Guizhou Province.*

Three Di xi *performers stand with swords raised to display the masks they will wear during the evening's performance. Long pheasant feathers have been attached to the ears of the masks to give each man a towering sense of height. Guizhou Province.*

figures with an assortment of demons and ghosts. Some of the performances were serialized over many nights, requiring that the audience return each evening to learn the fates of their favourite characters.

The enormous popularity of Chinese shadow theatre meant that it spread rapidly. By the thirteenth century it was well established throughout Southeast Asia and by the eighteenth century it had been carried to Europe, where shadow puppets are said to have inspired the art of the paper silhouette.

Itinerant Chinese puppeteers remain an expected feature at many county fairs and village markets, often comprising a single individual travelling by foot or donkey. Working from a cloth body-tent and wielding a collection of hand or stick puppets, the lone puppeteer plays out a series of simple dramas. The hand-crafted puppet heads are usually carved in wood by the puppeteer himself and brightly painted to represent a variety of heavenly, human and animal characters. Clothes for the earthly characters are constructed of rough homespun fabrics sewn or draped over wooden forms to represent the harsh life of the peasant. The garments of celestial beings or classical opera characters are typically dressed in elaborate silks and brocade robes, and crowned with a beaded headdress or tiara. Itinerant puppet shows are still widely popular in Shaanxi and Gansu Provinces, where they are performed during festival periods by semi-

A Han Dynasty rubbing from a carved stone depiction of the White Rabbit grinding the elixir of immortality, an image symbolic of the Moon Festival.

professional puppeteers, who help to maintain the vibrant and colourful folk traditions of the region.

Of all the celebrations enjoyed during the Chinese lunar year, the Mid-Autumn Festival is one of the most popular. Falling on the fifteenth day of the eighth lunar month, the mid-autumn, or 'Moon Festival' as it is commonly known, was originally a time to admire the full moon and recite poetry by its light. While the aspect of poetry reading may have fallen into decline, the festival is still highlighted by the exchange among family and friends of perfectly round *yuebing* ('moon cakes'), which symbolize the beauty of the moon and the perfection of the cosmos.

Folk legend ties the moon cake tradition to a secret uprising during the Yuan period, when rebels eager to overthrow the ruling Mongols concealed detailed plans of their rebellion inside the individual pastries. As the cakes were merrily exchanged, select participants were quietly informed of the coming uprising, which allowed them to unify their efforts and capture a strategic enemy stronghold.

Today, immense pride is taken in the making of moon cakes in elaborate wooden moulds. These bear auspicious phrases or intricate folk motifs, painstakingly carved in reverse by expert craftsmen well versed in the rich legends and symbolic imagery of the Moon Festival.

One of the most popular folk figures appearing during the festival is that of the Moon Goddess, Chang-e, represented by a women in long flowing gowns. Chang-e was the wife of Hou Yi who, armed only with a bow and arrow, saved China's peasants from drought by shooting down nine of ten suns which had appeared one day threatening to scorch the earth. Soon after, Chang-e secretly drank an elixir of immortality that had been given to her husband as a reward for his good deed. Rendered helpless, she slowly floated upward to the moon, where she became ruler of the lunar kingdom. At mid-month when the moon is full, it is said that Chang-e briefly meets her husband, who reigns over the solar realm, causing the moon to shine most brightly.

PAPER

*Warm water soothed my tired feet,
and cut paper was burned to revive my weary spirit*

– Adapted from Du Fu, *Song of Pengya*, AD 757

From earliest antiquity the Chinese people have expressed the hopes and fears of their uncertain lives through the simple depiction of the forces that guide their destinies. Tales of superhuman gods who were presumed to rule over periods of renewal and decay, fortune and famine, lej55d the ancients to develop rudimentary symbols in recognition of their supreme powers. Whether etched on ceramic pots or carved on secluded cliffs, these early markings were an attempt by agrarian people to predict and govern the mysterious meteorological and astrological manifestations affecting them. Their first expressions included an abundance of circular spinning fish designs and complex divinatory markings known as the *Ba gua,* or 'Eight Triagrams', which were associated with the deities Fuxi and Nüwa, the original creators of the material world. The early use of such pictograms on ritual offerings of grain and other staples was intended to placate the gods of wind and rain and to ensure abundant harvests free from pestilence and drought.

In time, the need to document a vision of the earth, complete with its turbulent cycles of creation and destruction, led them to create more complex and emotional renderings of the world around them. Life, death and the wish for immortality preoccupied the thoughts of the nobles, who ordered their funerary tombs prepared with all that they would need to provide an afterlife free of mortal concerns. Detailed paintings, discovered in tombs from the Western Han Dynasty, portray a dynamic world when gods were still believed to roam the earth and ferocious dragons with human heads and animal bodies were thought to inhabit the seas.

From the earliest attempts to give concrete form to a vast body of oral legends, distinct visual models emerged of the individual gods, whose benevolence was considered fundamental for a life of happiness and prosperity. In a ritual that evolved from primitive animal sacrifices, paper substitutes bearing likenesses of the gods were burned to show their deep respect. These representations, known as *zhima* ('paper horses'), grew from the conviction that winged horses acted as messengers between heaven and earth. Thus, the paper tributes were believed to

fulfil a similar function by transmitting the vision of the people to the heavens above. Their use gradually expanded from honouring the deities of wind and rain to the many other spirits overseeing every aspect of daily life. Some paper tributes were burned on auspicious days, such as the image of the hearth god, Zao Jun, whose smoky ashes rose from village chimneys each new year, but whose tribute was quickly replaced by a fresh copy to protect the family throughout the next twelve months. Other deities were burned during ceremonial exorcisms in an attempt to rid the home of hardship or disease.

Many of these beliefs continue to play an active role in the paper arts of today's rural Chinese. Although the earliest forms of spirit worship have long since vanished, the use of traditional paper tributes to ward off danger and celebrate the new year remains a popular and widespread practice. The tradition of posting colourful New Year prints *(Nianhua)* with images of fat cheerful babies holding symbolic offerings, or of dancing peasants celebrating bountiful harvests, is intended to welcome the New Year and engender good

A Yi minority home in rural Yunnan Province displays a pair of woodblock guardian prints on the front doors to drive away evil.

acute. Religious symbols that were once carved into stone or printed on strips of cloth as simple talismans grew into complex and detailed representations of heaven and earth. To accommodate these visions, an early form of paper, composed of bamboo and silk fibres, was introduced. This provided a welcome alternative to sheep-skin and papyrus, although – where the production of silk was not well established – yields were often small and the costs prohibitive.

Important refinements in the paper formula came during the Eastern Han Dynasty (AD 25–220) when a combination of ground bark, hemp and cloth rag was introduced by Cai Lun (d. AD 121), a minister of Imperial edicts and documents. The resulting paper proved practical and inexpensive, and its wide availability radically changed the development and dissemination of literature and the visual arts. In compensation for his discovery, Cai Lun was made Duke of Kaifeng and his paper subsequently bore the name 'Duke Cai's Paper'. The composition and the manufacturing techniques remained carefully guarded secrets and survived unchanged for centuries. Only in AD 751 did knowledge of the papermaking process begin to move westward when a group of skilled Chinese papermakers was purport-edly captured in Samarkand by Arab traders plying the Silk Road. When they were forced to reveal their secrets, the techniques were carried to the Moorish regions of Spain by 1150 and continued to spread throughout the rest of Europe during the next two hundred years.

By the Tang period (AD 618–906) engraved woodblocks were in regular use for the printing of both religious and secular images on paper. The earliest surviving example, known as the *Jin Gang Jing* ('Diamond Sutra'), dates from AD 868 and was discovered among other early

luck. Of the many paper deities in use today that honour individual gods, several are still accompanied by offerings of food, functioning in essentially the same manner as the tributes created thousands of years ago. Struck from hand-carved wooden blocks, each of these prints attempts to gratify the same forces that preoccupied the lives of their ancient forebears.

The legacy of China's paper crafts is as old as the invention of paper itself. As a result of a general literary and artistic awakening that occurred during the Western Han Dynasty (206 BC–AD 9), fertile minds began to blend primitive myth with new depictions of the everyday world. Ancient forms of spirit worship came head to head with the rational reforms of Confucianism, a religion grounded in historical experience. In this atmosphere of change the need for a flexible medium on which to relay these evolving ideas and images grew

The workshop of the traditional woodblock carver and printer, Tai Liping, showing a number of recently struck images in both colour and black and white. From the rafters hang collections of completed prints awaiting sale.

The major stages in papermaking as recorded in a seventeenth-century woodcut from the book The Exploitations of the Works of Nature. *First, lengths of bamboo were cut and soaked to loosen the tough outer layer. A pulp was then produced using ground and boiled bamboo, hemp and cloth rag. Next, a thin layer of the mixed pulp was lifted from a vat using a finely woven screen. The resulting sheet was pressed to release lingering moisture and smooth the surface before being applied to the sides of a wood-fired chimney for final drying.*

within the palace for the purposes of art education. At the same time, farmers' almanacs, containing notes on agricultural and medical matters, as well as auspicious days for planting and harvesting, became widely available in rural areas.

From surviving depictions of street scenes during this period, it is also clear that the practice of posting door gods had become well established. One of the earliest references to a printed deity used to protect the home may be found in *Writings on Meng Xi* by the Song Dynasty author Shen Kuo. In it he notes that the Imperial Court commissioned the printing of a portrait of the warrior Zhong Kuei to stand guard against lurking spirits and demons. According to legend, Zhong Kuei was a rural scholar who longed to attend the Imperial examinations in the hope of achieving the highest rank and the right to marry the Emperor's daughter. After being granted a powerful sword and sufficient money for the journey by a wealthy benefactor, Zhong Kuei set off to take the exams. Along the way he fell ill and in this weakened state was mercilessly attacked by demons who turned his face black and scarred his features. After coming highest in the examinations, but denied the Emperor's daughter as a result of his ugly appearance, Zhong took his own life, vowing revenge on the demons of the underworld that had destroyed his happiness. In honour of his courage and self-sacrifice, the image of Zhong Kuei may still be seen on the doors of many rural households, brandishing his sword in a challenge to any evil that might approach.

Documents from the Han Dynasty also tell of the brothers Shen Tu and Yu Lei, who captured unfriendly ghosts and fed them to tigers. Their likenesses were painted on peachwood panels that were hung over doors to ward off danger. In a similar legend, the Tang Dynasty Generals

Buddhist writings in the Thousand Buddha Cave in Dunghuang, Gansu Province. Conceived in the form of a scroll, the Diamond Sutra depicts a sermon by Sakyamuni, in which he extols the importance of tranquillity of body and mind. During the centuries that followed, the Chinese excelled in the art of block printing, producing important works in the fields of agriculture and medicine. Between AD 1101 and 1125 the Song Emperor Hui Zong commissioned the first woodcut catalogue, documenting the impressive bronze collection of the Imperial Palace. This work included both a pictorial inventory and instructions for its circulation

The Jin Gang Jing, *otherwise known as the 'Diamond Sutra', the earliest surviving woodblock print, dating from* AD 868.

Qin Qiong and Jing De were said to have been ordered by an aged and fearful Emperor to stand guard outside his bed chamber each night for a week. Noting that no demons had dared approach, they devised a plan to paint their likenesses on either side of the door but again hid in wait. Yet another week passed and no spirits appeared. Taken as proof of their deterrent power, these events led to images of Qin Qiong and Jing De being reproduced in woodcut versions ever since.

The posting of historical characters who have been immortalized as patron saints also remains a popular practice, reflecting the desire for spiritual and moral guidance in the daily activities and labours of tradesmen and peasants alike. Chinese woodworkers and carpenters have cherished the image of the peasant architect Lu Ban, who wandered the country applying his formidable talents where none had succeeded before him. Weavers continue to worship the patron saint Huang Daopo, who escaped an oppressive family life to learn and share with others many advanced techniques for spinning and weaving. And potters still look to the beneficent Fan Li to guide their hand and protect their kilns during the production of fine ceramic wares.

Today, only a few rural artisans have been able to maintain and preserve these printing traditions in their authentic form.

One of the most respected woodblock printers is Tai Liping. Working from a small, dimly lit studio attached to his ancestral home in Xiaoli village, Shaanxi Province, Tai effectively continues the practice firmly established by his family during the early years of the Qing Dynasty. His intense interest in the history of New Year prints and spirit images has led to his current effort to copy many of the family's ancient printing blocks, which have been irreparably worn or damaged by time. The continuity of tradition that Tai Liping represents in artisanal printing imbues his work with a special significance, making it avidly sought after by both local peasants and distant collectors.

Perhaps the most original and haunting woodblock designs originate with the minority people of Yunnan Province. Their high-contrast black and white compositions retain much of the primitive force and symbolic abstraction found in the earliest folk prints. The roughly executed images often display a profound disregard for anatomical correctness and include eerie composite beasts, winged deities and inanimate objects that are brought to life in keeping with the animist beliefs of the region. In these works, pictorial realism is always less of a concern than emotive appeal, which strives to flatter the gods or frighten away evil.

The use of woodblock printing is not solely confined to the production of New Year and spirit images. Traditional playing cards are also produced in this manner.

Referred to as 'page cards' during the Song Dynasty, they are printed on heavy-gauge paper and then cut into long strips for use in gambling games resembling Mah Jong. The shape and design of the cards varies widely from region to region, but most are eight to fifteen centimetres in length and feature boldly carved symbols or patterns in black, white and red. Some depict characters from historical novels, such as *108 Heroes from Liang Mountain.* Many rural playing cards are painted by hand, using simple stencilling methods whereby the colours are brushed over a cut paper pattern, imprinting the card stock beneath. This transfer technique has been in popular use for centuries and originated with the printing of folk motifs on textiles. Cut paper patterns also served as embroidery guides and constitute the earliest known shadow

puppets, which can be traced to Shaanxi Province. Their inspiration probably comes from ancient practices of creating decorative trimmings for the clothing and hair in materials such as gold and silver foil, silk, leather and even pressed bamboo. In the *Chronicles of the Chu State* it is noted that during the Liang Dynasty women greeted the arrival of spring with the cutting of elaborate coloured silks and gold foil finches which they wore in their hair. As the costs of such lavish decoration exceeded the resources of all but the most aristocratic classes, the common people were left to create similar decorations in paper.

Excavations along the Silk Road have produced examples of what are thought to be the first specimens of decorative paper cuts, dating to the Southern and Northern Dynasties. These include a pair of horses cut in a circular motif from mustard-coloured paper and a similar design featuring monkeys. The continued crafting of auspicious birds and animals today has come to be viewed as instrumental in the protection and prosperity of the family and home. Many of the paper cuts depict scenes from famous folk tales and bear descriptive titles such as 'The Whipping of Hong Niang' or 'Mice Eating Grapes'. The most recurrent images tend to be those of the twelve *sheng xiao,* or animals of the zodiac, which feature prominently among the decorations during their year of rule.

The ready availability of paper and the ease with which it is cut encourages quick, spontaneous expressions, without the complex materials or equipment required for other crafts. Equipped with a tiny pair of blackened steel scissors, girls as young as six years of age are initiated into the art of paper cutting in the presence of their accomplished elders. Many designs are cut in the inspiration of the moment, without a predetermined plan or sketch. Other themes, those that are regularly repeated,

A rural woman feeds her animals. A delicate paper cut from Ansai, Shaanxi Province, bordered by a heavy design of abstract, geometric and floral patterns.

make use of a master pattern which is placed on a fresh sheet of paper and held to a smoking oil lamp. When the smoke has amply penetrated the cavities of the original, it is removed, leaving a clear outline by which succeeding copies can then be cut.

As with the art of woodblock printing, the peak of creative paper cut activity corresponds to the yearly festivals and celebrations that mark the changing of the seasons. By far the most important continues to be the lunar New Year, often referred to as the Spring Festival, when for several days the Chinese clean their homes, prepare and exchange special foods and visit with family and friends. In Shaanxi Province colourful paper cuts known as *chuang hua*, or 'window flowers', are pasted on the heavily mullioned windows and doors of almost every home, as a welcome addition to the bleak northern winters and in anticipation of the arriving spring. The styles and characteristics of the decorative paper cuts may vary widely from region to region, but always correspond to one of two basic functions involving protective and curative properties, or aspects of fertility. Around these basic concepts many variations and nuances can be interpreted in accordance with a specific celebration or event. In Shaanxi the casting out of evil or sickness is achieved through the cutting of a human silhouette which is laid directly on the body of the afflicted. The paper cut is then removed and burned, and the ashes thrown into a bowl of water to be carried to the nearest crossroads, where the entire contents is emptied. Wedding decorations, which fall into the category of fertility themes, often depict young women with their hair tied in a bun, a symbol indicating the girl's willingness to marry. This well-known practice is repeated in an ancient Shaanxi folk saying:

Typical mullioned window of a village home in Shaanxi Province with its collection of fresh paper cuts. Such works are cut from colourful papers during idle hours and sold to visitors and friends.

My hand did not shake when I pinned up
  my bun.
Soon a fine suitor is likely to come!

The paper cuts of Shaanxi Province are generally coarse as a result of the less costly utilitarian grades of paper that are used there, while those of Guangdong are reputed to be the most delicate and refined, fashioned from painted metallic papers to create radiant and sparkling designs. Red is the colour that traditionally signifies happiness, and marriage paper cuts are often affixed directly to the wedding bed in a explicit wish for many children. The mother-in-law may also paste the figure of a tiger on the door where her daughter-in-law has just given birth, in a practice intended to scare away evil elements that may await the newborn child. Yellow,

Playing cards such as these feature simple, highly graphic designs, which are stencil-printed on heavy cardboard. Hebei Province.

green and multicoloured paper cuts announce the approaching spring and small paper brooms are sometimes hung from the trees to sweep away prolonged summer rains that may jeopardize the season's crops.

Paper cuts are also regularly pasted to lanterns, casting images that dance with the light of the flickering candle. Couples with sons born to them during the year may choose to hang a lantern in their ancestral hall or village temple during the 'Lantern Festival' on the fifteenth day of the New Year to announce officially the birth and symbolically introduce the baby to his ancestors in a ceremony that will assure his familial lineage. The general popularity of the Lantern Festival dates to the Song Dynasty, when competitions were held to reward the most inspired and original designs. These included intricately pleated geometric forms and giant swimming fish,

all proudly paraded through the village streets suspended from the tops of long bamboo poles.

Today, children in many parts of the country are still given painted rabbit lanterns identical to those depicted in ancient engravings. Attached to a wooden chassis fitted with primitive wooden wheels, the rabbits are pulled through the streets and courtyards, to the delight of the many elderly onlookers who remember this lingering tradition with fondness.

Although many of China's regional folk arts have shown a degree of resilience to the changing times, the fate of the paper crafts always seems particularly perilous, as they are constantly under attack by nature itself. Although materially strong, paper remains a physically vulnerable medium. Set in opposition to the primordial elements of both wind and flame, even the most carefully crafted lanterns eventually

succumb to nature's force. The colourful New Year images, posted to show respect and devotion throughout the year, also exhibit a fragile impermanence, since they are mercilessly bleached by the blazing summer sun.

The relative simplicity and ease of construction of many of China's arts and crafts do not make their demise easier to accept. Although their primary meaning is tied to the context of their ceremonial use, as outsiders we still attach to them an emotional or nostalgic value far greater than the intentions of their creator. Perhaps this is because many of the crafts enjoyed in China today represent similar traditions that our own cultures abandoned long ago. Our admiration of these simple objects brings to us a comforting degree of reassurance that the little things that once enriched our own lives still play a vital role in the lives of others.

The Crafts

(preceding page) Four decorative silver boxes with painted porcelain lids crafted from the broken remains of traditional vases and pots.
(large) 25 x 17 cm
(small) 7 x 6.5 cm

Stone bridge carvings in the form of the animals of the zodiac, which allow reflection on the cyclical passing of time. Pictured here are the ox, monkey, tiger, snake and (opposite) pig.

Four *shehuo* gourds embellished with opera and animal faces derived from the tradition of face-painting, which was practised on the thirteenth and fourteenth days of the lunar New Year. Often used as ladles, they are believed to drive away evil spirits and purify water as it is drawn from giant urns. Shaanxi Province. l. (longest) 8.5 cm

A pair of gourd cages make miniature worlds for singing cicadas. Each is carved with stylized floral motifs and fitted with a wooden top inset with a carved bone flower. d.8 cm

(opposite) Miniature gourd rattles finely engraved with scenes depicting popular folk legends, such as 'One Hundred Sons at Play'. Anhui Province. d.5 cm

(opposite) Bone necklace composed of stained, carved and pierced beads. Carved coins and a bat amulet engender good fortune. Kunming, Sichuan Province. l.37 cm

Carved ox bone pendants. One side shows two children catching bats under a tree, a symbolic reference to 'good fortune'; the other side bears the 'double happiness' symbol, commonly seen during weddings and other celebratons. Beijing, Hebei Province. h.5 cm

Group of Immortal or *Xian* figures in carved and stained ox bone. Individual pieces can be worn around the neck for guidance and good fortune or displayed in the home. Beijing, Hebei Province. h.4 cm

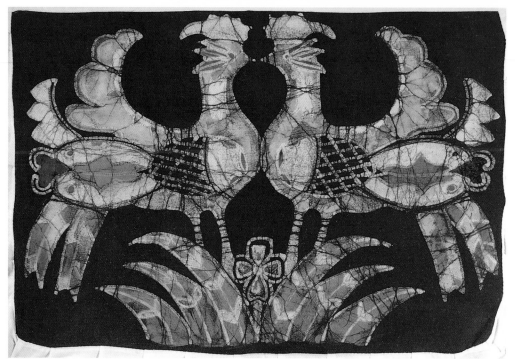

Multicoloured batik panel-print of two cocks. Shilin, Yunnan Province. 35.5 x 51.5 cm

Blue and white resist-printed cotton in butterfly, bat and cock motif. Kunming, Yunnan Province.

Red and blue resist-printed cotton in pomegranate and vine motif. Yunnan Province.

Detail of embroidery from Miao ceremonial clothing, featuring a boy riding a phoenix. Guizhou Province.

Detail of an embroidered waistband with fish motif. Bai minority, Yunnan Province.

Detail of embroidered waistband with butterfly and lotus design. Bai minority, Heqing, Yunnan Province.

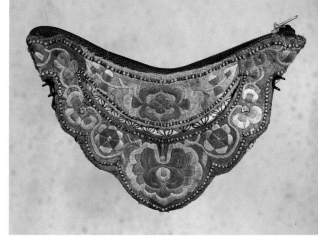

Embroidered Bai minority purses from Yunnan Province.

(clockwise from top left) Butterfly and flower design in twisted satin-stitch with black cotton piping and silk brocade banding. Shaping, Yunnan Province. h.11 cm; floral design in satin-stitch with decorative couching. Heqing, Yunnan Province. h.9.5 cm; satin-stitch floral design with decorative couching, possibly adapted from the decorative crown of a child's hat. Shaping, Yunnan Province. l.16 cm; couched appliqué flower design embellished with glass sequins. Jiangwei, Yunnan Province. h.10.5 cm

Embroidered Bai minority purse with floral design in satin-stitch with decorative couching. Heqing, Yunnan Province. h.9.5 cm

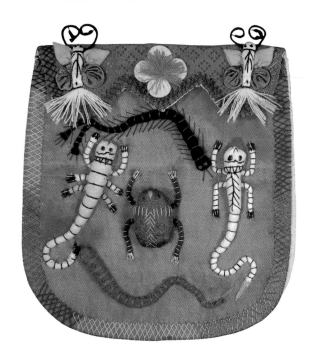

Embroidered purse with appliqué
creatures representing the 'Five Poisons'.
Xian, Shaanxi Province. h.13.5 cm

Small cotton bag with embroidered shoulder strap
featuring multicoloured cross-stitch embroidery.
Sanyi minority, Shilin, Yunnan Province. l.15.5 cm

Embroidered belt sash in satin-stitch butterfly and flower design, with silver couching on blue satin and additional cotton piping. Bai minority, Heqing, Yunnan Province. h.17.5 cm

Embroidered shoulder bags.

(from left) Black cotton bag with butterfly, fish and flower motifs. Hani minority, Shilin, Yunnan Province. h.34 cm; bag decorated with lotus flowers and stylized children, conveying longevity and abundant offspring. Bai minority, Dali, Yunnan Province. h.22 cm; woven cotton bag with *shan su zhu* nut decoration. Wa minority, Cangyuan, Yunnan Province. h.32 cm; natural cotton homespun and cotton velour with coloured ribbons and machine stitching. Hani minority, Shilin, Yunnan Province. h.38 cm

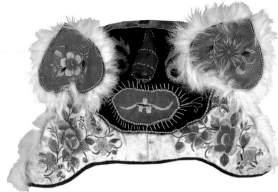

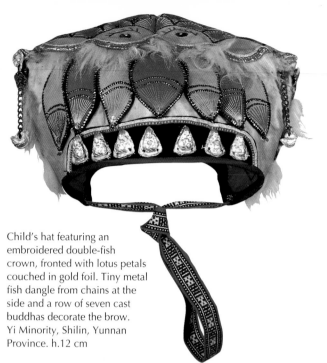

Child's hat featuring an embroidered double-fish crown, fronted with lotus petals couched in gold foil. Tiny metal fish dangle from chains at the side and a row of seven cast buddhas decorate the brow. Yi Minority, Shilin, Yunnan Province. h.12 cm

Child's tiger hat with appliqué face, embroidered flower and bird designs edged in rabbit fur and black cotton piping. Bai minority, Dali, Yunnan Province. h.17 cm

Embroidered and appliqué children's shoes with hand-stitched soles. *(top row from left)* Red velour with turned-up toe. Sanyi minority, Kunming, Yunnan Province. l.15 cm; red cotton tiger shoes with rabbit fur trim. Xian, Shaanxi Province. l.13 cm; black cotton pig shoes. Xian, Shaanxi Province. l.14 cm; brown padded brocade pig shoes. Lingtong, Shaanxi Province. l.15 cm; gold brocade tiger shoes edged with rabbit fur. Guangdong Province. l.13.5 cm; padded red cotton tiger shoes. Lingtong, Shaanxi Province. l.14 cm

A traditional *bei er bu,* or baby-carrier, with tie straps in heavy padded black velour, bearing embroidered floral motifs, butterflies, birds and rows of mice. The central lotus flower design is topped by a small male figure in honour of male progeny. Other embellishments include tiny metal sequins, chain-stitched borders and a quilted bottom panel with auspicious appliqué coin designs affixed with metal studs, believed to bring good fortune. Bai minority, Jiangwei, Yunnan Province. h.66 cm

White cross-stitched waist sash in geometric
butterfly and flower designs on black cotton.
Bai minority, Shaping, Yunnan Province.
l.190 cm

Ceremonial headdress in coloured satin
with machine-embroidered ribbons.
Yi minority, Shilin, Yunnan Province.
h.24 cm

Body sash of hand-woven cotton with fringed ends and tie strings. Nu minority, Kunming, Yunnan Province. l.390 cm

Two 'Hundred Birds' *Wushi yi*, or shaman coats, in heavily embroidered silk, worn during Miao ceremonies to exorcize evil spirits.

Padded charms of a boy and girl, traditionally hung on the doors of a new business to wish good luck. Chengdu, Sichuan Province. h.30.5 cm

Embroidered and stuffed fabric camel and tiger toys. Qian County, Shaanxi Province. h.14 and 17 cm

Child's bib featuring an upper panel embroidered with a large butterfly among flowers on black cotton. Lower panel embroidered with small peacock and peonies on blue satin. Tujia minority, Hubei Province.

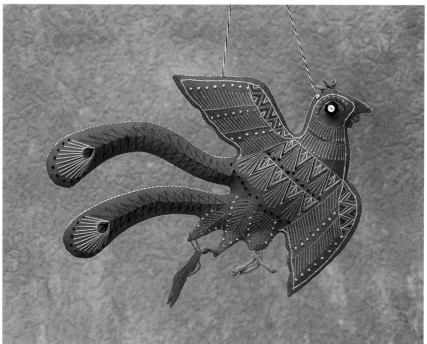

Embroidered purse in the form of a fish, symbolizing surplus or abundance. Qianyang, Shaanxi Province. h.23 cm

Padded and embroidered phoenix to bring happiness and good wishes. Qianyang, Shaanxi Province. h.17 cm

(*opposite*) Padded and embroidered double fish and lotus flower hanging. Qianyang, Shaanxi Province. h.48 cm

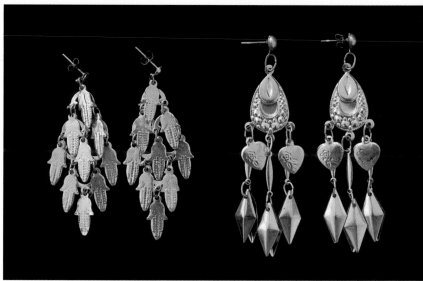

Dangling fish earrings in cast nickel alloy, signifying abundance. Yunnan Province. l.4 cm

(left) Stamped tin earrings in the shape of ears of corn, symbol of fertility and a plentiful harvest. Yunnan Province. l.8 cm. *(right)* Peach and diamond drop earrings in stamped tin. The peach is a common symbol for immortality. Yunnan Province. l.8 cm

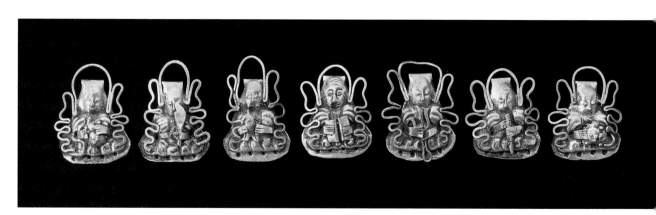

Repoussé *Xian* or 'Immortal' figures, intended for a child's hat, to lend guidance and protection. Each figure holds a symbolic object by which his character is commonly identified. Yi minority, Shilin, Yunnan Province. h.3 cm

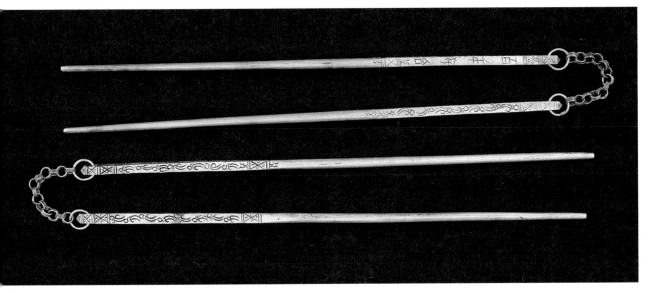

Two pairs of ceremonial chopsticks, typical of those presented at a marriage, engraved with cloud swirls and the inscription 'United for a hundred years'. l.21 cm

Ceremonial belt in *baitong*, with a repoussé peacock buckle and finely linked flowered bands. Shilin, Yunnan Province. l.84 cm

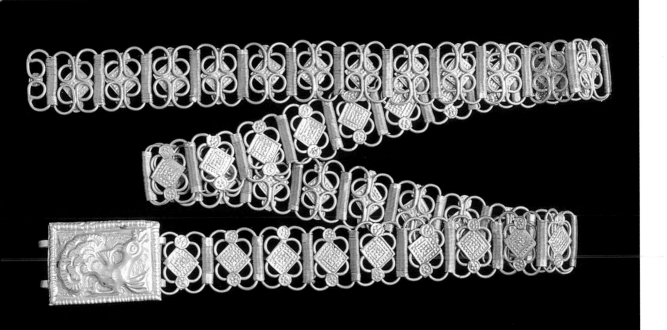

Three woman's rings in *baitong*. *(foreground)* Band with a central row of fine beads flanked by coiled and braided wire. Miao minority. d.2 cm. *(rear)* Two repoussé chrysanthemum rings with additional surface chasing and piercing. Yi minority, Yunnan Province. h.6 cm and 2.8 cm

Elegant cuff of braided and hammered silver. Miao minority, Dali, Yunnan Province. w.4.5 cm

Pair of repoussé bracelets in *baitong* with chased 'Empress' design of a phoenix and dragon. Yunnan Province. d.7.5 cm

Intricately woven bracelet composed of twelve twisted and braided wire filaments in silver-plated copper. The fineness of the weave produces an extremely flexible band with natural spring that can be easily opened and closed. Yi minority, Guishan, Yunnan Province. d.9 cm

A large *qiling*, with longevity bells dangling from its feet and tiny seeds hung overhead, makes a potent amulet for protecting and enriching the future of a male child while simultaneously wishing for more offspring. Yi minority, Yunnan Province. l.31 cm

Ornamental padlock necklace for a youth in *baitong*, bearing peach designs as symbols of longevity, and three small seeds suspended on tiny chains, an expression of the desire for further male offspring.
Yunnan Province. l.31 cm

Large ornamental padlock necklace in *baitong* suspended on a square link chain with tiny butterfly charms. One side bears a repoussé design of a *qiling* among peony flowers and the other the inscription 'A hundred years of long life'. Yunnan Province. l.32 cm

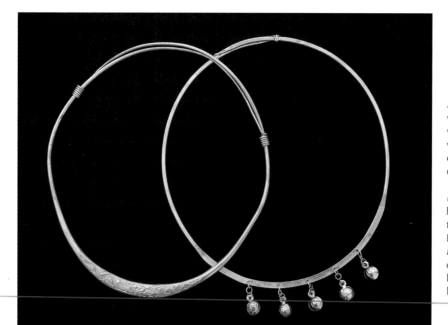

A hammered wire neckband in *baitong* with chased design of two dragons playing with a pearl. d.18.5 cm; wire neckband with a row of tiny bells stamped with the character *fu* for luck. Yunnan Province. d.18 cm

(opposite) (inner) Chased and pierced bracelet in *baitong* with suspended lotus flower locket. Hani minority, Yunnan Province. l.13 cm. *(outer)* Small flask in *baitong* with a repoussé design of chrysanthemum flowers hung on a round link chain. Bai minority, Yunnan Province. l.30 cm

Many varieties of stone necklaces are still made by classically trained artisans at the Beijing Jade Carving Factory, who take pride in overseeing the various phases of production themselves. From the initial selection, cutting and polishing, various grades of turquoise, jade and other semi-precious stones are fashioned into symbols of abundance and longevity, then strung on elegant silk cords, often finished with an 'endless knot' and fanciful tassles.

The richly veined stone bracelets of Huaqing Pool at the foot of Mount Lishan in Shaanxi
Province recall the simplicity and perfection of China's earliest amuletic jewelry. d.8.5 cm

Three red lacquer boxes carved with elaborate floral designs. The largest
lacquer boxes and vases often use a brass inner form for rigid support.
Beijing, Hebei Province. d.18 cm, 7 cm and 6 cm

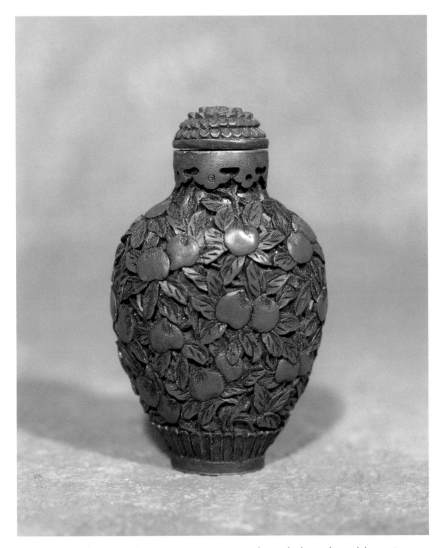

A carved lacquer snuff bottle bearing an intricate peach motif. The crafting of decorative snuff bottles in China dates from the Manchu conquest in 1644. Their overwhelming popularity within the Imperial Court resulted in the establishment of artisanal workshops in many provinces in order to satisfy the soaring demand. As a result, Guangzhou (then Canton) came to specialize in enamelled, carved ivory and coral bottles, Suzhou excelled in carved rock, while carved enamel versions were made in Beijing.
Beijing, Hebei Province. h.7.5 cm

Carved lacquer pendants bearing auspicious symbols for happiness and finished with silk tassels. d.5.5 cm and 2.8 cm

(top) The peculiar carving of these red lacquer animals is typical of the rural crafts of Sichuan, which draw their influence from the many primitive animal representations found in the region. Chengdu, Sichuan Province. h. (tallest) 7 cm

(above) Four flower and vine bracelets in carved red lacquer, often referred to as 'cinnabar'. Beijing, Hebei Province. d.7.5 cm

Black and red carved lacquer teapot with peony and leaf motif.
Beijing, Hebei Province. h.12 cm

Red and black lacquered tray bearing a mythical phoenix design, inspired by ancient lacquer vessels uncovered in archaeological excavations of the region.
Chengdu, Sichuan Province. d.31 cm

Red lacquer plates with ancient phoenix and 'spinning fish' motifs inspired by the painted pottery of Banpo.
Chengdu, Sichuan Province. d.19.5 cm

Round lacquered box with a gold inlay phoenix design, and a black lacquered box with abstract plant forms in polished silver inlay.
Chengdu, Sichuan Province. d.11 cm

A pair of rough, hand-modelled devil masks in unglazed clay. These are hung in rural homes in Sichuan Province to scare away intrusive ghosts and spirits. Chengdu, Sichuan Province. h.18–19 cm

Hand-modelled goat and ox, created in hearth-baked or sun-dried clay as simple folk toys or decorations for the home. Dali, Yunnan Province. h. (tallest) 9.5 cm

Painted clay tigers are renowned in and around the villages of Fengxiang County in Shaanxi Province. They are finished with symbolic flowers mounted to the ears and tails, which bob and sway as they are touched. Fengxiang, Shaanxi Province. h. (large) 38 cm, (small) 30 cm

Reclining clay lion and standing lion with spring mounted tail. Fengxiang, Shaanxi Province. h.6.5 cm

Opera figures in clay remain popular craft subjects. It is not uncommon to find the characters of an entire opera, rendered with exacting attention to authentic hairstyles and costumes. Beijing, Hebei Province. h.7.5 cm

Six of twelve painted clay animals representing the signs of the zodiac. The reigning animal during the year of one's birth has long been thought to be a dominant factor in determining character traits. Represented here are the tiger, horse, cock, ox, rat and dragon. Wuxi, Zhejiang Province. h. (tallest) 4.8 cm

Painted clay toy representing the 'Herd Boy Riding an Ox' who, in popular legend, is reunited with the Weaving Maiden on the seventh day of the seventh month. Fengxiang, Shaanxi Province. h.14 cm

(opposite) Press-moulded clay mask painted to resemble a famous Sichuan opera character. Chengdu, Sichuan Province. h.16 cm

Covered ceramic cricket box with brass pull. This type of box generally holds fighting crickets which are lifted from their grass beds with a small bamboo scoop during autumn festivities. Dingshan, Jiangsu Province. h.7 cm

Yixing clay teapot in the form of an edible bamboo shoot. Yixing, Jiangsu Province. h.8 cm

(opposite) Assorted clay wares, flower pots and planters at the ceramics market in Dingshan, Jiangsu Province.

Three beige-coloured teapots crafted in the form of a bell, a winter bamboo shoot with decorative bamboo leaf, and a *lao ling*, or caltrop. Dingshan, Jiangsu Province. h. (tallest) 12 cm

Artisanal teapots with calligraphic inscriptions in classic Yixing styles. Dingshan, Jiangsu Province. h.10 cm and 8.5 cm

(opposite) Large blue clay teapot with elaborate branch handle and bearing primitive pictographs. Dingshan, Jiangsu Province. h.40 cm

Porcelain vases painstakingly wrapped in fine hand-dyed bamboo splints. The patterns are reminiscent of early ceramic wares and take up to a month to complete. Chengdu, Sichuan Province. h. (tallest) 22 cm

Set of four woven bamboo nesting baskets with the inside bottom of the smallest bearing a hand-painted panda. Chengdu, Sichuan Province. d.7–16 cm

Three woven and pressed bamboo plates in geometric motifs bearing the characters for fortune and luck. Chengdu, Sichuan Province. d.26 cm

A pair of longevity and good fortune figures in wrapped bamboo over a wood core. Chengdu, Sichuan Province. h.13.5 cm

Set of twelve carved bamboo chopstick rests depicting the animals of the zodiac. h. (average) 3.5 cm

(opposite) Covered lacquer basket decorated with bamboo painting. Such baskets are made in every conceivable size, some with multiple stacking tiers. They are regularly used for the transport and storage of food and are often mounted with hardware to be carried on shoulder poles. Zhejiang Province. d.34 cm

Hand-painted bamboo butterfly fan. Butterflies represent advanced age and are often used as a symbolic wish for long life. Sichuan Province. l.26 cm

Paper fan with bamboo staves, embellished with famous characters from Sichuan opera. Sichuan Province.

Two painted bamboo peacock fans representative of dignity and beauty. In Chinese legend peacocks dance when they see a beautiful woman. Sichuan Province. l.30 cm and 10 cm

Scented boxwood fans with decorative piercing are popular with southern women during the warm summer months. Their natural perfume protects delicate clothing when tucked into a drawer for the winter. Chengdu, Sichuan Province. l.20 cm

A variety of hand-cut wooden combs from Wuxi, Jiangsu Province.
(clockwise from top left) Unpainted wood with heat-stamped bird and flower
designs. h. (largest) 7 cm; three combs painted with auspicious images: Shou
Xing, the God of Longevity, a young boy bearing a fish symbolizing the wish
for an abundance of high-ranking sons, and Chai Shen, the God of Fortune,
holding a *yuan bao* (gold ingot). h. (largest) 6.5 cm; hand-painted fish comb.
The Chinese word for fish, *yu*, is phonetically similar to that for abundance
or affluence. As a result, depictions of fish are generally meant to bestow
wealth. l.14 cm; pair of decorative wooden combs painted with dragon and
phoenix designs, symbolic of Man and Woman. l.11 cm; three brightly
painted butterfly combs with silk neck cords, potent symbols of longevity. w.
(largest) 9.5 cm

Two moulds carved in reverse, one depicting Chang-e, also known as the 'Moon Lady', and the other an intricate dragon and phoenix design symbolizing the union of man and woman.

Carved Bodhisattva in fragrant wood. This type of miniature reliquary is easily carried on the body or tucked into luggage for guidance and protection during travels. h.6.5 cm

Wooden 'Moon Cake' moulds bearing auspicious symbols are still used to form the delicate pastries that are the highlight of Mid-Autumn festivities, beginning on the fifteenth day of the eighth lunar month. Each province specializes in its own particular cake size, shape and preferred filling.

Carved and painted *Di xi* masks with elaborate headdresses often feature snakes or animal faces and tiny pieces of mirror. The *Di xi*, or 'Di Opera', is based on popular tales of combat that first took place under the Emperor Zhu Yuanzhang during the early Ming Dynasty. Masks such as these are therefore frequently embellished with moustaches and beards of human hair, and represent specific historical characters. Guizhou Province. h. (average, without hair) 32 cm

Nuo xi masks are usually carved with wild and contorted facial features to assist the local shaman in driving away evil.

A multicoloured woodblock print, glued to stable doors to protect the animals and ensure future prosperity. Jiangsu Province. 19.5 x 23 cm

A four-colour woodblock print by the artist, Tai Liping, featuring a pair of 'lucky boys'. Multicoloured images such as these use a series of individual woodblocks, one for each colour, which must then be perfectly aligned during the printing. Xiaoli village, Shaanxi Province. 33 x 43.5 cm

Multicoloured woodblock print
announcing the coming of spring.
Through a popular rendering
technique, the heads of five
children are transformed into ten
interconnected bodies. Here they
are surrounded by the animals of
the zodiac. Hebei Province.
33 x 23 cm

Woodblock print in honour of the Kitchen God, which is pasted near the hearth each year and burned on the last day of December. In a short ceremony, members of the family traditionally gather to watch the ashes rise up the chimney. It is thought that in this manner the spirits chained in the print will deliver a good report to the gods and further engender good health and prosperity for the coming year.
Sichuan Province. 25.5 x 14.5 cm

A regional hand-coloured woodblock print in honour of a household god. Local legends have mixed with popular themes over many centuries creating variations particular to each region. This one deals with the infidelity and misfortunes of a local landlord.
Shandong Province. 23.5 x 16.5 cm

Pair of hand-coloured woodblock prints depicting the Generals Qin Qiong and Jing De, who stood guard outside the bedroom of Emperor Tai Zong to protect him from evil. It was soon discovered that prints made in their likeness proved to be equally effective deterrents, and their images have been posted on doors throughout China ever since.
Hebei Province. 24.5 x 14.5 cm (each)

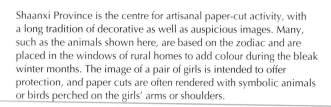

Shaanxi Province is the centre for artisanal paper-cut activity, with a long tradition of decorative as well as auspicious images. Many, such as the animals shown here, are based on the zodiac and are placed in the windows of rural homes to add colour during the bleak winter months. The image of a pair of girls is intended to offer protection, and paper cuts are often rendered with symbolic animals or birds perched on the girls' arms or shoulders.

The tradition of kite-flying in China can be traced to the Spring and Autumn period some 2,500 years ago. Prior to the first century AD kites were referred to as *zhiyuan*, or 'paper eagles', and many were outfitted with whistles that would sing as they flew through the air. Today the most famous are those made in Weifang, Shandong Province, where there is an annual festival, at which new kites are displayed and rival kite-flying teams compete for international recognition.

(opposite) Three bearded Beijing opera characters hand-painted on silk and fashioned into miniature kites. Beijing, Hebei Province. l.24.5 cm

(overleaf) Large hand-painted dragonfly kite. Weifang, Shandong Province. l.94 cm

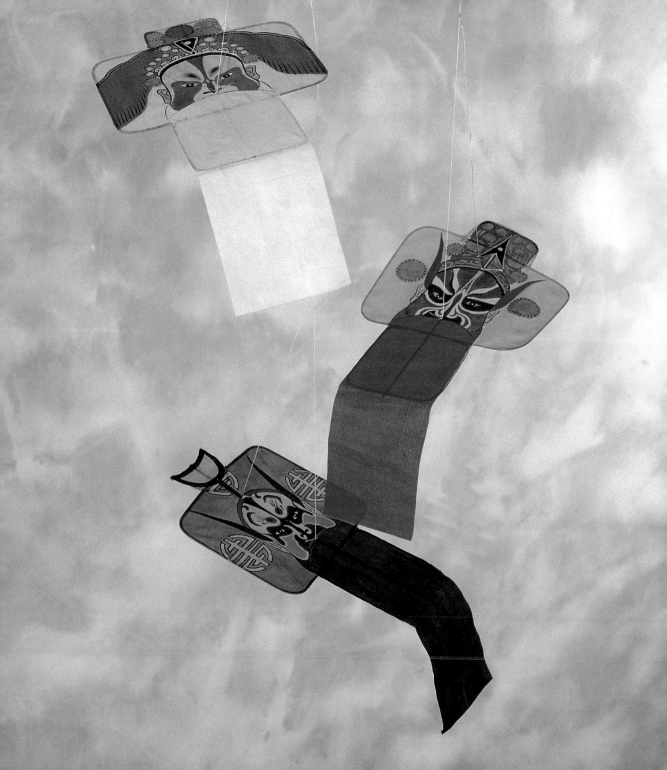

Map | 121

Collecting Chinese Arts & Crafts

There are few memories more rewarding after a trip to China than those attached to a hand-picked collection of its regional arts and crafts. From the initial discovery in an out-of-the-way place, through a bit of determined bargaining, careful packing and then the final struggle to return everything safely home, each object will carry with it a story indelibly etched in your memory. In a land as great and diverse as China, history and myth collide with amazing strength and imbue even the smallest items with an exotic personality all of their own. From Yixing teapots to hand-embroidered shoulderbags, China's diverse folk arts provide a lively and detailed account of an ancient culture undergoing tremendous change.

What you choose to collect is very much a matter of personal preference, influenced only by the places you will visit. Each province offers a distinctly different range of crafts, determined by the raw materials and traditions of that area. As in many countries catering to increasing numbers of tourists, however, you must usually wade through a sizeable amount of institutionalized craftwork to arrive at something truly special. For the many travellers to China who are bound to the larger cities for reasons of time, language or physical comfort, uncovering that special something need not be a daunting task. Given that you are not restricted by an impossibly fast tour, it is entirely feasible to build a wonderful and varied collection of Chinese arts and crafts with a little serious searching.

As any collector knows, finding good examples of a particular craft on demand is not an easy order. In China, it is immensely easier to find something where you are than to try to find where it is. Therefore, if you see an unusual item that pleases you, buy it. Procrastination often leads to disappointment as, chances are, you will not have the time to return for it later. The extremely reasonable prices of Chinese arts and crafts often lead to an oddly distorted economizing, and declining to buy because of a small hesitation over the cost will only bring you sighs of regret once you are home.

Chinese cities and towns are renowned for their unique speciality shops, which cater to a single type of product or craft. Although the rapidly changing face of urban China has forced many traditional merchants to relocate, most cities harbour 'old towns' around which antique and craft dealers now congregate. Many cities also boast unofficial flea markets where locals and tourists regularly congregate to buy, sell and trade an amazing diversity of new and old goods.

For those visiting only major Chinese cities or those who want a quick overview of the breadth of Chinese crafts, the large government-run 'Friendship Stores' and curio shops offer the best chance to see a variety of work from around the country. Although they are shunned by many as commercial tourist havens, the searching eye can always turn up an unusual item or worthy antique unlikely to be found elsewhere. Collectors should note, however, that in a country where replicas and fakes bearing stamps of authenticity inundate the antiques market, a good rule of thumb for purchases of seemingly older goods is to buy what appeals to you, at a price that you will be happy with, regardless of an object's true age or provenance.

Collectors wishing to buy rural craft work will have no trouble finding groups of eager hawkers at popular tourist sites. If you want to avoid both the costs and the herd mentality of commercialized excursions, consider boarding a bus intended for Chinese sightseers. They offer destinations often overlooked by Western eyes and at lesser-known sites the opportunity of buying goods directly from those who make them. This is particularly rewarding in China's numerous minority regions, where the easing of travel restrictions has been met with an increase of good-quality minority crafts. Visitors to these areas will always find a large selection of hand-embroidered clothing, textiles and artisanal jewelry offered for sale at attractive prices and may be able to negotiate visits to private homes to see the crafts being made. It should be noted that such visits are still the exception and must be arranged with some delicacy. Expectations by both parties are often set too high. Remember that cordial invitations are normally a pretext to sell the local products, regardless of their quality or appeal, and villagers may appear offended if you do not buy something. Conversely, tremendous discretion should also be used by the foreigner in attempting to purchase anything other than what is specifically intended for sale.

In many remote areas of China, the presence of an outsider is still greeted with great curiosity by the entire village, but even with a skilful Mandarin speaker, the local dialects are often impossible to penetrate. The Western visitor to rural homes should be prepared to find harsh living conditions and keep in mind that photography of the people without their consent may not only be viewed as an invasion of privacy, but also violate local religious beliefs and ingrained superstitions.

For those who do not have the opportunity to travel to mainland China, do not despair! Many fine examples of China's indigenous crafts may be found in major cities throughout the world. Hong Kong is an excellent source for many mainland arts, as well as having a specialized arts and crafts industry all of its own. Those seeking antique items and curios should head to Hong Kong's Western district. Both Hollywood Road and Cat Street feature a number of shopping emporia devoted to handmade works of art. Man Wa Lane is also filled with unique crafts and is particularly well known for its carved Chinese 'chops' (seals). Similarly, the Hong Kong Arts Centre in the Wanchai district features a shop devoted to contemporary Asian arts and crafts and Queen's Road East is legendary for its rosewood cabinetmakers and rattan furniture shops. Lovers of jade should prepare to be overwhelmed by the Jade Market in Kowloon's Yau Ma Tei district. Seven days a week, 450 vendors offer a dizzying array of China's most cherished stone, from simple jewelry to intricately carved keepsakes and collectibles.

The many ethnic Chinese populations spread across the globe have also developed urban 'Chinatowns' in many European and North American cities, which constitute a centre for traditional Chinese commerce and culture. Although it is unlikely that you will find much in the way of rural handicrafts outside China and Hong Kong, more popular arts and crafts are always in abundance. Since the 1960s Gerrard Street has been the focal point for London's Chinese community. Within just a few short blocks, a lively mix of boutiques offers a large assortment of traditional ceramics and table-wares, folk-art prints, paper kites and bamboo calligraphy brushes. During the Chinese New Year, lavish celebrations, featuring winding dragon dances, compete with temporary street stalls selling holiday foods and festival crafts to usher in a year of increased prosperity and good health. Similar celebrations are held in Manchester, England, where a large Chinese presence has led to the creation of numerous shops and galleries, featuring changing displays of Chinese folk arts and crafts.

San Francisco's Chinatown is perhaps the best-known Asian community in the United States, with a long and established history of social and cultural programmes that help to maintain the values and traditions of many generations. Grant Avenue forms the major axis of the community, off which you will find streets lined with herbal pharmacies, Cantonese reading rooms, commercial trading companies and decorative arts shops. Similar communities exist in Chicago, whose principal thoroughfare is dominated by a mammoth Chinese archway, and in New York, whose Chinatown is now home to over 100,000 residents. Centred around Mott Street and extending down Canal, Pell, Bayard, Dowers and Bowery Streets, New York's busy Chinese quarter echoes with an exotic mix of regional dialects; narrow sidewalks overflow with imported

groceries, crates of fragrant teas and stacks of earthenware vessels. Mixed in among the open doorways are shops devoted to colourful lacquer and bamboo crafts, traditional clothing and jewelry.

Each of the cities mentioned above also has numerous upscale boutiques catering for the rise in popularity of Chinese folk art, furniture and collectibles. To purchase items of greater age or historical importance, or to obtain an accurate identification or valuation of objects already in your collection, seek a reputable dealer of Asian antiques or consult an established auction house.

No matter where you find rare or unusual Chinese collectibles, great care should always be taken in their preservation and display in the home. Even among seemingly similar goods, handmade arts and crafts are never identical. Slight variations in material, form, colour or inspiration make each piece unique and in that sense irreplaceable. In addition, every medium has its own particular properties that can be adversely affected by sudden changes in climate, exposure to sunlight or inappropriate cleaning methods. Lacquer and wood items may develop cracks in an overly dry environment, textiles are subject to fading and their impermanent dyes are often easily damaged. Wood-based papers will inevitably fade and yellow, and ceramic glazes may respond poorly to the rigours of daily use. Do not hesitate to seek professional advice for the proper caring of such items whenever you are uncertain.

Listed below are those minorities that are particularly well known for their special festivals and traditional arts and crafts.

Bai *Population 1,590,000.* Eighty per cent of the Bai live in villages in the Dali Bai Autonomous Prefecture in Yunnan Province. Originally Buddhists, they developed as skilful builders and carvers, as represented in several pagodas at the Cangshan Temple in Dali, dating from the Tang Dynasty. Bai opera, known as *chui chui,* displays traditional Han influences combined with regional folk music and dancing. An annual festival during the third month of the lunar calendar provides an ideal opportunity to view the Bai women in their traditional costumes and jewelry when they gather at the foot of Mount Diancang, located to the west of Dali. The Bai still practise the decorative art of tie-dyeing and

examples may be bought in the many neighbouring villages bordering Lake Erhai.

Bouyei *Population 2,540,000.* The largest minority in Guizhou Province, the Bouyei are experts at embroidery and batik, and sing many traditional songs in praise of these skills. During festivals the Bouyei engage in a courting game known as the 'Flowered Bag Toss' whereby dozens of young people, arranged in facing rows, randomly throw colourful handsewn pouches back and forth until a preferred recipient is finally chosen.

Dai *Population 1,020,000.* The Dai reside primarily in the southern Yunnan region of Xishuangbanna, bordering Burma, Vietnam and Laos, an area sometimes referred to as the 'Home of Peacocks'. Originally followers of Hinayana Buddhism, they gradually mixed these beliefs with elements of shamanism. The Dai have successfully maintained many of their ancient celebrations, including the 'Water Sprinkling Festival', in which young men and women splash each other with basins of water in the belief that it will wash away sickness and introduce a prosperous New Year.

Dong *Population 1,510,000.* Spread across Guizhou, Hunan and Guangxi Provinces, the Dong have long depended on rich resources of timber, tong oil, lacquers and varnishes for their economic survival. Their innovative wooden homes and Drum Towers are also highly regarded among architectural historians. Homespun cloth is frequently used in the making of traditional Dong clothing, and embroidery and needlework are learned from a very early age in preparation for the sewing of elaborate waist sashes, which the women customarily present to their fiancés as a symbol of their devotion.

Hani *Population 1,250,000.* Principally located in the southwestern border areas of Yunnan Province, the Hani are composed of more than twenty sub-groups, who are often referred to by their distinguishing elements of dress. Such is the case with the Aini sub-group, who are called 'round head' or 'flat head' Aini in reference to the differing shapes of their ceremonial headdresses. The clothing of Hani women may be easily identified by the tradition of embellishing the chest with rows of small silver studs. Hani lands are especially rich in tin ore, as well as natural shellac, which is widely distributed for use in handicrafts. The famous Pu'er tea is also cultivated by the Hani people.

Jingpo *Population 93,000.* The majority of Jingpo live in the Dai Jingpo Autonomous Region in Yunnan Province. Originally practitioners of fetishism, the Jingpos engaged in complex sacrificial rites during sowing, harvesting, weddings and funerals, aimed at appeasing the spirits believed to be chained in the many birds, animals, rocks and trees that surrounded them. Superstition still abounds and the crafts produced today regularly reflect their ancient beliefs. Jingpo women are renowned for wearing multiple silver neck chains decorated with sequins and silver bells, which are believed to offer protection from evil.

Lahu *Population 304,200.* The Lahu people live primarily in Lancang County on the southwest border of Yunnan Province. Their homes are built on stilts, with the space underneath serving as shelter for their animals. The Lahu have historically been polytheists and continue to erect carved wooden totems in honour of their many gods. Traditional Lahu handicrafts include ironwork, weaving, bamboo articles and pottery. Their patterns are distinctive in the frequent use of triangular shapes, which create strikingly bold patchwork effects when used in clothing and textile designs.

Li *Population 1,110,000.* Hainan Island off the coast of southern China is home to the Li people, who settled there 3,000 years ago during the late Shang Dynasty. Originally a matriarchal society, the Li practised animism and were believers in witchcraft. Li women have long been prolific weavers, with skills that helped to develop China's earliest cotton spinning and weaving techniques. They have also retained an extensive knowledge of herbal medicine, which is dependent on many of the island's indigenous plants.

Lisu *Population 481,000.* The Lisu inhabit the Nujiang Lisu Autonomous Prefecture in northwestern Yunnan Province and favour homespun linen and printed cotton clothing. Long aprons, decorated with panels of embroidery, seashells, nuts and stones, continue to be made by the Lisu women and headdresses

and necklaces are often adorned with strands of red and white glass beads.

Maonan *Population 38,100.* The Maonan minority live in a sub-tropical area in the north of the Guangxi Zhuang Autonomous Region. Although they are primarily an agricultural people, a significant portion of their income is derived from woven bamboo handicrafts such as hats, pillows and matting. In addition, the Maonan are skilled craftsmen known for delicately carved articles in wood and stone.

Miao *Population 7,390,000.* The Miao are scattered widely across the southwest provinces of China and form the fifth most populous ethnic minority. Regular trade practices with the Han were established as early as the Song Dynasty, bringing important economic stability to their villages. Fond of singing and dancing, the Miao have succeeded in maintaining strong folk traditions in literature and the visual arts. In addition, they have preserved their wealth of skills in weaving, cross-stitch, embroidery and batik, decorating each piece of clothing with stylized flower, bird and animal motifs. These designs are drawn from a vast historical collection which originally helped to identify their geographic origins. Their impressive jewelry crafts, which feature large ornamental crowns, have become the highlight of an annual festival that serves to unite the Miao of different villages.

Nu *Population 23,200.* The Nu inhabit the Nujiang Lisu Autonomous Prefecture in western Yunnan Province, where they maintain cottage industries in handmade goods consisting primarily of wood and bamboo. Surplus goods were used as barter with neighbouring communities from an early period, helping to establish a regional trading network. Until the introduction of commercially produced cotton cloth the Nu preferred to wear homespun linen. Nu women achieved some renown for their special coral and glass bead necklaces.

Shui *Population 286,500.* Inhabitants of southern Guizhou Province, the Shui are famous for their rich history of folk arts and oral literature. Particularly vivid are their narrative poems and ballads, which are accompanied by drums, gongs and a variety of traditional instruments. Shui

embroidery is especially cherished, as is their work in batik, paper cuts and wood carving. The Shui are distinctive dressers, preferring black and blue gowns, aprons and turbans, which are all richly embroidered.

Tujia *Population 5,700,000.* The Wuling Range of western Hunan and Hubei Provinces has been home to the Tujia, whose name literally means 'local folk', since the early Five Dynasties period (AD 907). They are descendants of an ancient tribe known as the Ba dating back three thousand years. After early contact with the Han culture, the Tujia developed skills in metal smelting, spinning and weaving. This has led to a clothing style bearing a close resemblance to Han garments of the Qing Dynasty, which are further embellished with intricate embroidery designs. Their exotic patterned quilts, known as *xilanlan hua bu*, originate as cotton brocades which are woven on the back-strap loom.

Yi *Population 6,570,000.* Although scattered over four provinces, the single largest community is located in the Liangshan Yi Autonomous Prefecture in Sichuan Province. An ancient people, the Yi can be traced to ancestors who lived during the second century BC. Originally practitioners of polytheism, they also merged elements of Taoism, Buddhism and ancestor worship. The Yi maintained strong ceremonial rituals for the dead, often involving carved memorial tablets cut in the shape of figures which were then buried in caves.

Zhuang *Population 15,480,000.* China's largest ethnic minority is concentrated in the mountainous area of the Guangxi Zhuang Autonomous Region. The Zhuang are practitioners of polytheism and ancestor worship, with a recorded cultural history extending over two thousand years. As early as the Tang Dynasty (AD 618–906), the Zhuang were involved in the production of rich brocades, for which they became legendary. The Zhuang continue to produce new and imaginative brocade designs today, woven of natural cotton warp and dyed velour weft. At the beginning of spring, they host a singing festival in which traditional improvised antiphonal singing and 'cross-examination' singing are still performed.

CHRONOLOGY

Neolithic Cultures

Central Yangshao	c. 5000–3000 BC
Gansu Yangshao	c. 3000–1500 BC
Hemudu	c. 5000–3000 BC
Daxi	c. 5000–3000 BC
Majiabang	c. 5000–3500 BC
Dawenkou	c. 4300–2400 BC
Songze	c. 4000–2500 BC
Hongshan	c. 3800–2700 BC
Liangzhu	c. 3300–2250 BC
Longshan	c. 3000–1700 BC
Qijia	c. 2250–1900 BC

Early Dynasties

Shang	c. 1500–1050 BC
Western Zhou	c. 1050–771 BC
Eastern Zhou	
Spring and Autumn	770–475 BC
Warring States	475–221 BC

Imperial China

Qin	221–207 BC
Han	
Western Han	206 BC–AD 9
Xin	AD 9–25
Eastern Han	25–220
Three Kingdoms	
Shu	221–263
Wei	220–265
Wu	222–280
Southern Dynasties	
Western Jin	265–316
Eastern Jin	317–420
Liu Song	420–479
Southern Qi	479–502
Liang	502–557
Chen	557–589
Northern Dynasties	
Northern Wei	386–535
Eastern Wei	534–550
Western Wei	535–557
Northern Qi	550–577
Northern Zhou	557–581
Sui	589–618
Tang	618–906
Five Dynasties	907–960
Liao	907–1125
Song	
Northern Song	960–1126
Southern Song	1127–1279
Jin	1115–1234
Yuan	1279–1368
Ming	1368–1644
Qing	1644–1911

Republican China

Republic	1912–1949
People's Republic	1949–

SELECT BIBLIOGRAPHY

Bartholomew, Terese Tse. *I-Hsing Ware*. New York: China Institute in America, 1977.

Beijing Academy of Art and Crafts. *A Brief History of Chinese Art & Crafts (Zhong guo gong yi mei shu jian shi)*. Beijing: People's Art Publishing House, 1983.

Berliner, Nancy Zeng. *Chinese Folk Art*. Boston: Little, Brown and Company, 1986.

Clunas, Craig. *Chinese Furniture*. London: Victoria and Albert Museum, 1988.

Dai Gangyi and Guo Youmin. *Shaanxi Folk Arts*. Hong Kong: Sinminchu Publishing Company, 1988.

Den Guanghua. *Nuo and Religious Art (Nuo yu yi shu zong jiao)*. Beijing: Chinese Cultural Union Publishing House, 1993.

Den Qiyao. *The Clothing with Ornamentation of Ethnos: A Cultural Sign (Min zu fu shi: yi zhong wen huao fu hao)*. Kunming: People's Publishing House of Yunnan, 1990.

Eberhard, Wolfram. *Dictionary of Chinese Symbols*. London: Routledge & Kegan Paul, 1986.

Ecke, Tseng Yu-ho. *Chinese Folk Art in American Collections: early 15th through early 20th centuries*. New York: China Institute in America, 1976.

Fu Gongyue. *Old Photos of Beijing*. Beijing: People's Fine Arts Publishing House. 1989.

Garrett, Valery M. *Chinese Clothing: An*

Illustrated Guide. Hong Kong: Oxford University Press, 1994.

Garrett, Valery M. and Szeto, Naomi Yin-yin. *Children of the Gods: Dress and Symbolism in China*. Hong Kong: Urban Council, 1990.

Gyllensvärd, Bo. *Chinese Gold, Silver and Porcelain: The Kempe Collection*. New York: The Asia Society, n.d.

Huang Tsai-lang, ed. *Arts and Crafts from the Republic of China*. Taibei: Council for Cultural Planning & Development, 1986.

Jian Feng, ed. *Yan'an Papercuts*. China: The People's Fine-Arts Publishing House, n.d.

Jin Zhilin. *Aesthetic Features of Chinese Folk Art: The Good Luck Dolly*. Paris: Librairie You-Feng & Musée Kwok On, 1989.

Knapp, Ronald G. *China's Vernacular Architecture*. Honolulu: University of Hawaii Press, 1989.

Kuwayama, George, ed. *Ancient Mortuary Traditions of China*. Los Angeles: Los Angeles County Museum of Art, 1991.

Li lu-lu. *Chinese Traditional Folk Festivals (Zhong guo min jian chuan tong jie ri)*. Nanchang: Jiangxi Art Publishing House, 1992.

Li Zehou. *The Path of Beauty. A Study of Chinese Aesthetics*. Beijing: Morning Glory Publishers, 1988.

Lu Pu, ed. *China's Folk Toys*. Beijing: New World Press. 1990.

Ma Yin, ed. *China's Minority Nationalities*. Beijing: Foreign Languages Press, 1989.

Meng Xian and Guo Hui. *Chinese Minority Customs and Folklore (Zhong guo shao su min zu feng su yu chuan shuo)*. Hebei: South Sea Publishing House, 1991.

Minick, Scott and Jiao Ping. *Chinese Graphic Design in the Twentieth Century*. London: Thames and Hudson, 1990.

National Minority Costume in China. Wai Yin Club. Hong Kong: Joint Publishing Company, 1985.

Pan Guanghua. *Chinese Miao Customs (Zhong guo miao zu feng qing)*. Guizhou: Guizhou Minority Publishing House, 1990.

Piper, Jacqueline M. *Bamboo and Rattan: Traditional Uses and Beliefs*. Oxford: Oxford University Press, 1992.

Qiu Huanxing. *A Cultural Tour Across China*. Beijing: New World Press, 1992.

— *Folk Customs of China*. Beijing: Foreign Languages Press, 1992.

Rawson, Jessica ed. *The British Museum Book of Chinese Art*. London: British Museum Press, 1992.

— *Chinese Ornament: The Lotus and the Dragon*. London: British Museum Press, 1994.

Stepanchuk, Carol and Wong, Charles. *Mooncakes and Hungry Ghosts: Festivals of China*. San Francisco: China Books and Periodicals, Inc., 1991.

Tao Yuanlong. *A Source Book of Lucky Patterns (Ji xiang tu an zi liao)*. Shanghai: Shanghai Picture Publishing House, 1989.

Tait, Hugh, rev. ed. *7000 Years of Jewellery*. London: British Museum Press, 1989.

Thorp, Robert L. *Son of Heaven: Imperial Arts of China*. Seattle: Son of Heaven Press, 1988.

Tregear, Mary. *Chinese Art*. London and New York: Thames and Hudson, 1980.

Wang Hengfu, ed. *Miao Costume (Miao zhuang)*. Beijing: People's Art Publishing House, 1992.

Wang Lianhai. *A Brief History of Chinese Folk Toys (Zhong guo min jian wan ju jian shi)*. Beijing: Beijing Art and Crafts Publishing House, 1991.

Wang Shucun. *Le Papier Fetiche: Le culte des dieux à travers les estampes folkloriques*. Beijing: Editions du Nouveau Monde, 1991.

— *One Hundred Chinese New Year Folk Paintings (Zhong guo min jian nian hua bai tu)*. Beijing: People's Art Publishing House, 1988.

Wang Yarong. *Chinese Folk Embroidery*. Hong Kong: The Commercial Press, 1985.

Wang Yu-wen. *Folk Art*. Hebei: Heibei Fine Arts Publishing House, 1990.

Watt, James C.Y. *The Sumptuous Basket: Chinese Lacquer with Basketry Panels*. New York: China Institute in America, 1985.

Wilson, Verity. *Chinese Dress*. London: Bamboo Publishing Ltd., 1990.

Wu Shan, ed. *A Dictionary of Chinese Arts and Crafts (Zhong guo gong yi mei shu da ci dian)*. Nanking: Jiangsu Art Publishing House, 1988.

Yan Hong-shu and Wang Zhu-zhen. *Chinese Pictorial Folk Art (Zhong guo min jian tu xing yi shu)*. Shanghai: Shanghai Bookstore Publishing House, 1992.

Yang Dejun, Ma Yisheng, Huang Minchu and Jin Xiaobai. *Articles of Personal Adornment (Shen shang shi pin)*. Yunnan: Cultural Relics Publishing House, 1991.

Yang Xue-qing and An qi. *An Introduction to Folk Art (Min jian mei shu gai ren)*. Beijing: Beijing Art and Crafts Publishing House, 1990.

Zhang Bingde, ed. *Guizhou Folk Batiks (Guizhou chuan tong la ran)*. Guizhou: Guizhou People's Publishing House, 1994.

Zhang Daoyi. *The Art of Chinese Papercuts*. Beijing: Foreign Languages Press, 1989.

Zhang Weiwen and Zeng Qingnan. *In Search of China's Minorities*. Beijing: New World Press, 1993.

Illustration Acknowledgments

Except where otherwise noted below, all photographs are those of the authors.

Colour photographs: Karel Steiner: 2, 6, 99, 119, 120. Liu Yung: 46, 47. Additional thanks to: Ikat, Paris, and Phoenix Bookshop, Paris, for the loan of numerous Chinese calligraphy materials featured on page 6; and to Asiatides, Paris, for access to their stock of Chinese baskets and moon cake moulds, which are included on pages 107 and 111.

INDEX

Colour plate page references are given in **bold** type, black and white illustration pages in *italic*.